Calvin and the Sabbath

Calvin and
the Sabbath

Richard B. Gaffin, Jr.

Mentor

ISBN 1 85792 376 6

Published in the Mentor imprint in 1998
by Christian Focus Publications,
Geanies House, Fearn, Ross-shire,
IV20 1TW, Great Britain.
Printed in Great Britain by J. W. Arrowsmith Limited, Bristol

Contents

Jean

In gratitude to God for all the many Sabbaths spent together

Preface

This volume, originally a Master of Theology thesis completed under the supervision of Professor John Murray at Westminster Theological Seminary in the academic year, 1961-62, has been thoroughly rewritten here for greater clarity and readability, but with only slight modifications in basic format and substance (apart from the concluding Evaluation in chapter 5, which, in places, has been revised and expanded). At a distance of some 36 years, its analysis, conclusions, and critique, I believe, are, for the most part, still sound.

Interaction with the modest amount of pertinent secondary literature that has appeared in the intervening years is largely confined to footnotes. I have also included some primary source materials in French, originally inaccessible to me.

My thanks to Malcolm Maclean, Managing Editor, and Christian Focus Publications for their commitment to this project, and to the Board of Trustees of Westminster Theological Seminary, Philadelphia for a study leave during the first semester and winter term, 1997-98, in part, to complete it.

In recent months, as I have prepared the manuscript for this volume by word processing, with the ease this technology affords for making corrections, moving material, adding and editing footnotes, checking spelling, etc., I have become keenly aware as I had not before, in contrast, of the magnitude of my wife's efforts, when those many years ago now, with our firstborn less than a month old (and without ever complaining), she so competently deciphered my often illegible handwriting and typed the original 200 plus page manuscript – with two carbon copies required, on an old (nonelectric) Smith-Corona (younger readers may have to have these details explained to them!). Now, at length, I am thankful to be able here to acknowledge that labor of love, along with so many others before and after too often taken for granted.

Westminster Theological Seminary, Philadelphia
July, 1998

Introduction

Calvin and the Sabbath. Devoting an entire book to a topic like this may seem questionable to some. For them, the meaning of the fourth commandment and Sabbath keeping are largely concerns of a bygone era offering little more than an appeal to their historical curiosity. For others, however, who acknowledge the abiding claim of the fourth commandment on their lives, our topic should have great practical interest.

It has to be said, however, that even among the latter an attitude toward the Christian Sabbath or Lord's Day exists that can only be described as ambivalent or even neglectful. In many Christian communions, it appears, the texture of Sunday observance is more often than not determined by traditionally accepted mores that have long since had obscured whatever Scriptural basis they enjoy. Moreover, a high degree of deviation from these mores is usually tolerated.

This attitude is puzzling, especially when the teaching of Scripture is taken into account, along with the fact that often those who neglect the Sabbath will acknowledge, when pressed, that the fourth commandment, as part of the Decalogue, ought to be treated with the same seriousness as the other nine. In fact, no commandment is more strictly enforced in the Old Testament, and in the New Testament, contrary to widespread belief, none is more highly regarded by our Lord. It would seem, then, that complacency in the matter of keeping the Lord's Day is to be explained, in larger measure, by the failure to reckon adequately with the relevant Biblical teaching.

The question of Calvin's views first came to my attention in the effort to become familiar with the history of debate on the Sabbath. Two things soon became apparent. First, widespread disagreement has persisted about what Calvin meant where he has expressed himself concerning the Sabbath. Consequently, he has been cited as a favorable authority on the Sabbath question for views that not only differ but clearly conflict with each other. That the usually perspicuous and incisive Calvin could be made to do service for mutually exclusive positions appeared to me to be highly improbable. Clearly one side, if not more than one, was failing to do justice to his views. Second, considering Calvin's towering stature and the weight of any appeal to his authority for many, it seemed worthwhile to deal with this anomalous state of affairs and, if possible, to arrive at some resolution.

This study proposes primarily to listen attentively to the Reformer of Geneva on the question of the Sabbath and then, more briefly, to evaluate that teaching in the light of Scripture. My hope is that this effort may serve in its own way to rekindle an appreciation of the splendor of the Sabbath idea in God's word and an awareness of continuing obligation to the fourth commandment. Faithful and joyful Sabbath-keeping, we should not forget, is among the most concrete ways for the church to witness to a world full of turmoil and unrest, as never before or at least as much as ever, that there does indeed "remain a rest for the people of God" (Heb. 4:9).

Chapter 1

Background

To facilitate our investigation of Calvin, two matters deserve at least brief attention: the spectrum of viewpoints on the Sabbath/ Sunday question, especially those emerging beginning with the Reformation, and the state of Sunday observance on the eve of the Reformation.

Summary of Theories Regarding the Sabbath or Lord's Day[1]

First to be mentioned are two views that represent opposite extremes. Neither has ever been maintained consistently for any great length of time, but both have continued to reappear periodically and reassert their influence.

The *antinomian* view[2] was prevalent among certain groups of the Anabaptist wing of the Reformation. Based on the premise of a sharp antithesis between law and gospel, it held that those in Christ no longer have an obligation to keep the ten commandments. The fourth commandment, therefore, has been abolished. The Sabbath no longer exists, much less the obligation to keep it. Observing the Lord's Day flatly contradicts New Testament teaching that all distinctions of times and seasons are abolished; every day is the Lord's Day.

The *seventh-day Sabbatarian* view is the polar opposite of the antinomian view. Strangely enough, it also appears in sixteenth century Anabaptism. In fact, according to Hessey,[3] there is good evidence that it arose as part of a conscious reaction to antinomian tendencies. The basic argument is that the believer's duty, as was Christ's, is not to do away with the law but to fulfill it. The fourth commandment is thus seen to bind New Testament believers in all of its Old Testament rigor. They must observe it on Saturday, often in all its Jewish strictness. This view, though it still appears in some Christian denominations, involves a virtual repudiation of the impact of Christianity on the weekly Sabbath.

A second theory or, more accurately, group of theories may be described as *ecclesiastical*, or, as its exponents generally prefer that it be called, Dominical.[4] These views all agree in maintaining that the fourth commandment and the Sabbath are strictly Mosaic in origin. They were mandated by God at the time of the Exodus as a special provision for the nation of Israel. Consequently, when the Old Testament economy came to an end, the obligation to the fourth commandment ceased and the Sabbath disappeared. The Lord's Day or Sunday, on the other hand, is a distinctive ordinance of the Christian church. It is not a Sabbath, nor is it the successor to the Sabbath. It is in no way dependent upon the fourth commandment for its sanction.

The only real difference of opinion that exists among the adherents of this view has to do with the question of the rationale or ultimate authority for the Lord's Day. One of two basic answers is usually given. Some are quite frank in saying that there is no other basis than an ordinance enacted by the church sometime during the first part of the second century or, at the earliest, toward the very end of the first century. Others, feeling that something as important as the Lord's Day can hardly be maintained on such an uncertain basis as the action of the church, assert that the sanction for the Christian observance of Sunday is at the very least an apostolic ordinance or perhaps even an unrecorded directive of Christ. They liken its sanction to what they consider to be the basis for infant baptism.

The Dominical view is that maintained by the Anglican Church almost from its beginning to the present. It received its classic expression by Hessey and others during the last century. Those who hold to it insist that although public worship is an integral part of the proper observance of Sunday, the day has been set aside primarily for physical and mental rest and recreation.

Thirdly, we come to those theories commonly known as *Sabbatarian*. Here the distinctive and basic element is that the fourth commandment is not merely a piece of Mosaic legislation but rather, along with the other elements of the Decalogue, is an expression of a creation ordinance. The weekly Sabbath, therefore, is not merely a Jewish institution and has not been abrogated by the coming of the New Testament dispensation. Its observance is universally and perpetually binding. In fact, the Sabbath had a place before the fall.[5] Another distinctive characteristic of this theory is that, with the advent of Christ, the day for observing the Sabbath has been changed from the seventh to the first, without repudiating the language or changing the force of the fourth commandment. A variety of arguments are offered in support of this change of day.

The question that most often divides Sabbatarians concerns the relation of the Old Testament Sabbath to the fourth commandment, a question vitally related to the practical problem of observing it. What in its ancient observance was determined by the intrinsic demands of the commandment and what was merely peculiar to its temporary theocratic administration? Of even greater importance has been the debate whether or not there is a ceremonial, that is, purely Old Testament, element in the fourth commandment itself, which has been abrogated with the advent of Christ. Sabbatarian views rose to prominence immediately after the Reformation and were strongly advocated by English Puritanism during the seventeenth, eighteenth, and early nineteenth centuries.[6] In the United States Sabbatarianism held a prominent place in the life of most major denominations until well into the nineteenth century. It has been rapidly disappearing ever since. Followers of this view usually consider proper Sabbath observance to consist in spending the whole time either in public worship or private acts of devotion; "rest for worship" is the controlling principle.

Even this brief sketch of viewpoints enables us to see the important and critical problems that must be addressed in discussing the meaning of the fourth commandment. Is the Sabbath a creation ordinance and therefore universally and perpetually binding, or is it simply part of the Mosaic legislation that passed away with the coming of Christ? What is the relation of the Christian celebration of Sunday to the Old Testament Sabbath? Is it valid to say that the former is the direct successor to the latter and that both receive their sanction from the fourth commandment? What is the essence of the Scripture's teaching regarding the Sabbath? Is it primarily a day of rest or a day of worship? Is there necessarily a conflict between these two emphases when they are considered in the light of the Biblical data? Although it is not within the scope of this study to deal with such questions formally, we will find ourselves confronted with them repeatedly. For, as we will see, the same questions challenged Calvin for an answer.

The State of Sabbath or Lord's Day Observance on the Eve of the Reformation

That, along with Calvin, Luther and others are called "Reformers" underscores the importance of seeing them in the light of their times. Both in what they did and what they wrote, these men must always be seen from the basic perspective of reaction to and reform of certain trends in doctrine and practice that at that time dominated Christendom. Commonplace as this observation may be, it is nonetheless one that may be lost sight of when we involve ourselves in the sheer volume of material from their pens. It especially bears reminding when our area of research is limited to something as specific as Calvin's views on the Sabbath.

It is not within the scope of this study to dwell at any great length on the general condition of the Roman Catholic church at the beginning of the sixteenth century. Commandments and schemes of human invention, no matter how well intentioned, had almost entirely obliterated the free gospel of Christ. Personal, vital communion with God, mediated directly by the word and Spirit, within the fellowship of the church, had been displaced by a hierarchical arrangement that dominated and regulated peoples' lives by an *ex opere operato* dispensing of sacramental grace.

It will be useful here, however, to notice in some detail the effect this hierarchical system had on the observance of Sunday. It is not entirely clear how Sunday was celebrated in the very early centuries of church history nor how in that period the Sabbath and its relationship to the Lord's Day were viewed.[7] There can be no doubt, however, concerning the state of affairs that began to develop in the church toward the end of the fifth century.

One of the less salutary effects of the formal Christianization of the Greco-Roman world, which began to take place with the issuance of the Edict of Milan (AD 313), was the inclusion of many, within the ranks of the faithful, for whom professing Christian faith was nothing more than empty words. The erstwhile pagan now became the nominal Christian, with predictable results. The vigorous body of Christ, previously tested and refined by the fires of persecution, that body that had stood out so unmistakably against the world, now became increasingly enervated, its witness blunted and obscured. The negative effects of Constantinian toleration were hardly negligible. As many of the medieval sects put it, the date of the Edict marked the "Fall" of the church, the beginning of its "Babylonian captivity."

Among the concessions the church made to the pagan world about it was a failure to take a clearly defined stand on the matter of festivals and religious holidays. Such celebrations had played an important part in pagan worship. But their religious significance is only part of the picture. For the average person, the common laborer, those festivals provided the only outlets for relaxation and diversion from an otherwise dreary and grinding existence. Without doubt, for many, if not most, the social aspects of these holidays far outweighed the religious.

Obviously this need for diversion still existed after Christianity superseded paganism, so that what apparently happened is not surprising. Since a religious basis had always served to sanction these festivals, now, similarly, a basis for festivals was sought in the Christian religion, giving whatever religious overtones were involved in their celebration a Christian rather than a pagan flavor. Although the influence of individual clergy was undoubtedly at work in the formation and maintenance of many of these early post-Edict festivals, it is important to note that they developed sporadically and locally. About them the official voice of the church was at first silent.

For reasons that need not be gone into here, the system of festivals that began to appear in the life of the church during the fourth and fifth centuries did not limit itself. Rather, as time passed, the number of holy days proliferated to a point where the church was no longer able officially to ignore them. Eventually it was felt necessary to determine which festivals were to be observed, and to define clearly the principle by which some holidays were to be sanctioned and others excluded as unworthy of Christian observance.

The search for a solution to this problem ended in what amounted, in effect, to a return to the provisions of the Old Testament economy. From its earliest days the church has been aware of an analogy between certain ordinances of the Old dispensation and institutions of the New. For instance, baptism was seen, however obscurely, to be related to circumcision. Beyond that, the church also went on to say, with regard to the matter of festivals, that the celebrations of the New Testament era should correspond to the ceremonies of the Old Testament. It was maintained that each one of the feasts of Israel had its counterpart in one of the holidays sanctioned by the church. This principle was variously expressed throughout the medieval period. We find it enunciated at a later point by someone as eminent and representative as Thomas Aquinas, "The Sabbath has been changed to the Lord's Day, as festivals of the new law replace other festivals of the old."[8]

The Christian observance of Sunday thus came to be based solidly upon Old Testament Sabbatarian grounds. Whether this particular identification was proper is not our concern here. What is important to note is that keeping the Lord's Day became integrally related to a system of ecclesiastically sanctioned legalism that rivaled any exercise of Pharisaic ingenuity. As the medieval period progressed, the true meaning of the Lord's Day almost disappeared, and the complexion of its celebration became increasingly colored by the legalistic system of which it was a part. The following citations make this assessment clear. They are taken, for the most part, from penitentials and synodical decisions and so reflect, probably more accurately than any other source, the pervading character of Sunday observance among the common people and laity.

The chief concern of the clergy seems to have been to prohibit work and fasting on the Lord's Day. The reason for prohibiting the latter stemmed from teaching of the ante-Nicene Fathers, for whom the Christian Sabbath, being a memorial to Christ's resurrection, is a day of joy. Accordingly, fasting and a kneeling posture for prayer, among other things, were discouraged as inconsonant with a joyful observation of the day.[9] *The Old Irish Penitential* (c. 800) states: "Anyone who fasts on a Sunday through carelessness or austerity does a week's penance on bread and water."[10] According to *The Penitential of Theodore* (690),

> But if on account of negligence anyone fasts on the Lord's Day, he ought to abstain for a whole week. If he does this a second time, he shall fast for twenty days; if afterward forty days.... If he fasts out of contempt for the day, he shall be abhorred as a Jew by all the Catholic churches.[11]

Prohibitions against Sunday work are similarly severe. *The Confessional of Egbert* (c. 950-1000) states, "Those who work on Sunday: these men the Greeks first admonish with words; if they do it again, then some of their property is taken from them; on the third offense they either scourge them or bid them fast for seven days."[12]

The Judgment of Clement (c. 700-750) prescribes:

If through negligence anyone does work on Sunday, either bathes himself, or shaves, or washes his head, he shall do penance for seven days; if he does it again, he shall do penance for forty days; and if he does it through contempt of the day and will not amend, he shall be cast out of the Catholic Church, as a Judas.[13]

According to *The Milan Penitential* (c. 1565-1582), one of the injunctions based on the third (fourth) commandment is that "He who does any servile work on the Lord's Day or on a feast day shall do penance for seven days on bread and water."[14]

Most of the above quotations reflect the situation in the early part of the medieval period. This situation, however, continued to intensify as time passed. As the church hierarchy strengthened its domination over the life of the individual, so the prescriptions regulating conduct on the Lord's Day increased both in number and minuteness. The following two lengthy quotations amply illustrate the nature of this trend. *The Laurentian Penitential* (c. 1200) has the following to say about the Lord's Day and its observance:

We decree the observance with all reverence of all Lord's days from evening until evening, and abstinence from illicit work, that is, that there be no gainful trade, nor a tribunal in which anyone is adjudged to death or punishment, unless for the sake of making peace. We also determine according to what the Lord hath commanded in the Law, that servile work be not done on the Lord's days, as my father commanded in his synodical edicts, that men shall neither carry on rural labors – the cultivation of vineyards, or the planting of hedges, or the setting out of groves or the felling of trees – nor the assemblage to the tribunals; nor shall trading take place, nor hunting be engaged in. There are three tasks requiring acts that may be done on the Lord's day: Provisioning a hostelry with bread, the care of work animals, and, if specially needful, the carrying of someone's corpse to the burial place. Woman shall not make woven work on the Lord's day; they shall not wash the head; they shall not sew garments together, nor pluck wool. It is not permissible to scrutch flax or to wash a garment or to shave the crown – in order that honor and repose may in every way be accorded to the Lord's day. But they shall come together from all sides to the celebration of masses and shall praise God for all the benefits which he designed to bestow upon us in that day. On the Lord's day it is not permissible to sail and ride for business in connection with any tasks, nor to make bread, nor to bathe, nor to write; for if anyone projects or carries on work, he shall do penance for seven days. The washing of the head may be done in case of sickness. If any offerings are permitted on the Lord's day, they ought to be made on Saturday by people who are fasting. If anyone fasts on the Lord's day, he shall fast for a whole week.[15]

Admittedly there are certain salutary emphases in this and other penitentials, such as the basic concern to limit work in order that there be freedom for all to worship. It is important to keep in mind, however, that in the final analysis all these regulations are part of sacramental system, where observing them was believed to have a part in determining an individual's state of grace.

It would be difficult to find a better example of the arbitrary and picayune spirit that eventually characterized regulations for observing the Lord's Day than the injunctions of Tostatus, Bishop of Avila, during the fourteenth century. His commentary on Exodus 12 includes the following stipulations, among others:

If a musician wait upon a gentleman, to recreate his mind with music, and they are agreed upon certain wages, or he be only hired for a present time, he sins in case he play or sing to him on Holy Days (including the Lord's Day), but not if his reward be doubtful or depend only on the bounty of the parties who enjoy his music.

A cook that on the Holy Days is hired to make a feast or to dress a dinner, commits a mortal sin; but not if he be hired by the month or year.

Meat may be dressed upon the Lord's Day or the other Holy Days, but to wash dishes on those days, is unlawful – that must be deferred to another day.

A man that travels on Holy Days, to any special shrine or saint, commits no sin, but he commits sin if he returns home on those days.

Artificers which work on these days for their own profit only, are in mortal sin, unless the work be very small, because a small thing dishonoreth not the Festival.[16]

Such, then, was the character of Lord's Day observance that emerged in the Roman Catholic Church during the medieval period. To be sure, there were those who rebelled against it. Isolated voices from among the clergy protested that no matter how the church tried to justify itself, the system of festivals, of which Sunday observance was a part, amounted to nothing else than a return to Judaism. More vigorous reaction characterized some of the sects. The Petrobussians in the eleventh, the Waldensians in the thirteenth, and the Lollards in the fourteenth century distinguished themselves by going to the lengths of abolishing not only fasts and festivals, but any distinction of days as well.[17]

But the above citations reflect the nature of Lord's Day observance typical on the eve of the Reformation. A day whose true significance had been almost entirely obscured by the encumbrances of an ecclesiastically sanctioned soteriological legalism – that was the Sabbath familiar to Calvin and others as they began their task of reform.[18]

References

1. See J. Hessey, *Sunday, Its Origin, History and Present Obligation* (London: Cassell, 1889), pp. 4-13 for a fuller discussion as well as extended bibliographic material relating to these theories; in the literature appearing since 1962, R. Bauckham, "Sabbath and Sunday in the Protestant Tradition," in ed. D. Carson, *From Sabbath to Lord's Day* (Grand Rapids: Zondervan, 1982), pp. 311-41. It bears emphasizing that I intend nothing more here than the briefest sketch of the basic strands in various theories.

2. This and subsequent designations of views are not original with me.

3. *Sunday*, p. 258.

4. W. Trevelyan, *Sunday* (London: Longmans, Green, 1902), p. 12.

5. This aspect, i.e., the pre-fall Sabbath, is often neglected in discussions about the fourth commandment.

6. The classic creedal expression of this view, no doubt, is found in the Westminster Standards: Confession of Faith, 21:7-8; Larger Catechism, 115-22; Shorter Catechism, 57-62; see as well the section, "Of the Sanctification of the Lord's Day," in The Directory for the Public Worship of God, also produced by the Westminster Assembly.

7. Cf. J. Gilfillan, *The Sabbath* (Edinburgh: Andrew Eliot and John Maclaren, 1861), pp. 378-91, where he seeks to show from their writings that the Fathers based the observation of the Lord's Day on the fourth commandment. However, Hessey, *Sunday*, pp. 23-87 appeals to virtually the same data in trying to prove the opposite, i.e., that for these men, the celebration of Sunday bore no relation to the Old Testament Sabbath. The origin and nature of Sunday observance, including its relationship to the Sabbath, in the early church continues to be debated; among more recent discussions, see R. Bauckham, "Sabbath and Sunday in the Post-Apostolic Church," *From Sabbath to Lord's Day*, pp. 251-98; R. Beckwith and W. Stott, *This Is the Day: The Biblical Doctrine of the Christian Sunday* (London: Marshall, Morgan and Scott, 1978), esp. chapters 5-13; W. Rordorf, *Sunday* (trans. A. Graham; Philadelphia: Westminster, 1968 [German original, 1962]). Rordorf has published, with translation and brief annotations, the pertinent materials from the first to the sixth centuries, in *Sabbat und Sonntag in der Alten Kirche* (Zürich: Theologischer Verlag, 1972) [= *Sabbat et dimanche dans l'Église ancienne* (Neuchâtel: Delachaux et Niestlé, 1972)].

8. "Sabbatum mutatur in diem Dominicum similiter alliis solemnitatibus veteris legis novae solemnitates succedunt" (cited by Hessey, *Sunday*, p. 90).

9. See H. Huber, *Geist und Buchstabe der Sonntagsruhe* (Salzburg: Otto Muller, 1958), pp. 49-54. This work is a thorough historical-theological study of attitudes toward the Sabbath from the beginning of the church to Aquinas.

10. J. McNeill and H. Gamer, *Medieval Handbook of Penance* (New York: Columbia University Press, 1938), p. 159.

11. Ibid, p. 194.

12. Ibid, p. 247.

13. Ibid, p. 272.

14. Ibid, p. 366.

15. Ibid, pp. 352-53.

16. Hessey, *Sunday*, pp. 91-92.

17. Hessey, *Sunday*, pp. 93 ff. gives a brief treatment of this negative reaction to the church's system of festivals, as well as relevant bibliographic material.

18. For a more recent treatment of the medieval period, see the survey of R. Bauckham, "Sabbath and Sunday In the Medieval Church In the West," *From Sabbath to Lord's Day*, pp. 299-309, and the literature cited there.

Chapter 2

Theological and Confessional Writings

Calvin was born in the northern French town of Noyon, located in the province of Picardy, on July 10, 1509. He died in Geneva on May 27, 1564.[1] During a lifetime of service to Christ, first at Geneva, then at Strasbourg, and finally, again, at Geneva, both by his preaching and writings, he was used to unleash forces for the greater good of the church. To him, perhaps more than any other human figure, the truly biblical emphases of the Reformation stand as a monument.

Understandably, among those who consider themselves heirs of the Reformation, appeal to Calvin constitutes a formidable witness in matters of theological debate. If for no other reason, then, the importance of our subject begins to emerge. The question of the meaning and obligation of the fourth commandment, which has provoked controversy in the church from its earliest days, has been no more heatedly argued than in Protestant circles during the past several centuries, and in those debates the teaching of Calvin has been cited as faithfully representing the teaching of Scripture.

What is surprising and even perplexing in this situation is not the appeal to Calvin's authority, but that more often than not, Calvin is cited by opposing sides in support of their respective opinions. He is made to do service for mutually exclusive points of view. According to Hessey, arguing from the writings of the Reformers (including Calvin) in defense of the Dominical view,[2] "Sabbatarians indeed those eminent men were not. They were utterly opposed to the literal application of the Fourth Commandment to the circumstances of Christians. They scarcely touch upon the commandment, except to show that the Sabbath has passed away."[3] Theodor Zahn expresses himself similarly,

He [Calvin], however, speaks about this matter in his exposition of the third[4] commandment only in order to show that the Christian celebration of Sunday has nothing to do with this commandment, and to refute "the prattle of the Sophists," who teach that the ceremonial regulation in the third commandment, namely the hallowing of the seventh day of the week, has been abolished but that the celebration of one day in seven is to be maintained as its moral content.[5]

Assertions like these clash with citations from authors who find in Calvin and the other Reformers support for the view that the weekly Sabbath commandment remains in force. Among a set of propositions that James Gilfillan seeks to prove is the following: "The Reformers believed the Sabbath to have been appointed by God at the creation for all time."[6] Patrick Fairbairn brings to a close his lengthy discussion of the Reformers' views on the Sabbath by noting that they

held that the Fourth Commandment strictly and morally binds men in every age to set apart one whole day in seven for the worship and service of God. They all held the institution of the Sabbath at the creation of the world, and derived thence the obligation upon men of all times to cease every seventh day from their own works and occupations. Finally, they held it to be the duty of all sound Christians to use the Lord's Day as a Sabbath of rest to Him.[7]

This contradictory state of affairs only becomes more confusing when we consider the approach taken by some in the Reformed tradition. Both Abraham Kuyper and Voetius before him are frank in maintaining that Calvin is guilty of basic inconsistency when he states his views on the Sabbath. According to them, in his exposition of the fourth commandment in the *Institutes of the Christian Religion*, he teaches that the day the church chooses for worship is a matter of indifference, while in his commentary on Genesis he says that God has appointed one day in seven to be observed perpetually by all as a day of worship. On the one hand, Voetius argues that the *Institutes* reflect Calvin's settled point of view and makes no effort to account for the teaching of the Genesis commentary. Kuyper, on the other hand, maintains that the teaching of the *Institutes* represents Calvin's earlier point of view, that the material in the Genesis commentary, which first appeared in 1554, gives a later and truer statement of his position, but that, for some inexplicable reason, in the last (1559) edition of the *Institutes* he left his statements from the earlier editions intact and failed to give expression to the change of mind that had taken place some five years earlier.[8]

Louis Praamsma arrives at the same basic conclusion as Voetius and Kuyper but goes beyond them in providing a plausible accounting for the conflict between the *Institutes* and the Genesis commentary.[9] That conflict, he holds, resulted from the different apologetic motives animating Calvin. In the *Institutes* his attention was directed against Rome and its legalistic observation of days.[10] In his concern to keep the free grace of the gospel unencumbered, he overstated himself in the direction of releasing believers from the obligation to any observation other than what they might choose to keep voluntarily.

On the other hand, in the Genesis commentary, his remarks have in view certain groups of Anabaptists, who denied that the Scriptures taught a Sabbath rest and even worked on Sunday like the other days of the week. Here he stresses that the Sabbath is a creation ordinance. Consequently, against Rome he denies that the observance of Sunday is based on a creation ordinance, while against the Anabaptists he affirms it.

Apart from a consideration of the interpretation that Praamsma gives to the pertinent data in Calvin, a couple of factors may be noted that indicate some basic difficulties with his approach. First, the alleged difference between Calvin's apologetic interests in the *Institutes* and in the Genesis commentary must be seriously questioned. The teaching of these sources will be considered in detail below, but for the present it may be noted that in his remarks in the *Institutes*,

Calvin clearly has Anabaptists as well as Roman Catholics in view.[11]

A second factor is a presumptive consideration drawn from the character of Calvin's writings as a whole. As Praamsma himself puts it, "... he was a very meticulous and fair-minded exegete."[12] If there is a consensus on anything among Calvin scholars, including those who are unsympathetic, it is that he was consistent and straightforward in presenting his ideas. To conclude that he is guilty of contradicting himself requires the strongest possible evidence, proof that will stand the test of evaluation in the light of all of his writings. Whether such evidence exists is a question we will take up later.

As the preceding discussion shows, a proper consideration of Calvin's teaching on the Sabbath cannot consist in simply evaluating his statements. Important and rewarding as the task of evaluation may be for furthering an understanding of the meaning of the fourth commandment, the more basic question that demands our attention is historical in character. Before criticism and evaluation can be undertaken, a clear conception of what Calvin in fact taught has to be obtained, something that so far does not appear to have happened. Our immediate concern, then, will be to present and gain an understanding of all those places where Calvin makes comments pertinent to the Sabbath/Sunday question.

The material to be considered may be divided into three categories: (1) the teaching of the *Institutes*, both the definitive edition of 1559 and the earliest edition of 1536; (2) the teaching of a catechism and a short creedal statement; and (3) the teaching of the commentaries.[13] In this chapter we will examine (1) and (2), which are more theologically oriented.

This ordering of the material as well as the manner of treating it, I should make clear, indicate a certain bias. A full and careful statement of the teaching of the *Institutes* will be our point of departure, with the remaining materials considered in that light. The propriety of that procedure is justified by the original design of the *Institutes*; as is generally recognized, they are a comprehensive and systematic presentation of Christian truth. The student of Calvin has the distinct advantage of being able to begin with what amounts to a thorough statement of his views. Only the most compelling considerations, such as in this case do not appear to exist, would dictate grounding our study in anything other than the *Institutes*. That does not mean, however, that the other data will not be given their due, or the overall accuracy of our conclusions compromised.

The Teaching of the *Institutes*

Eight different editions of the *Institutes*, all in Latin, appeared during Calvin's lifetime.[14] From most of these, French translations were made, some by Calvin himself. The first edition appeared in 1536 at Basel. As the prefatory letter addressed to Francis I of France makes plain, its broad purpose was apologetic. It was intended as a statement and defense of the views of many of Calvin's friends who, at that time under the wave of persecution that had forced Calvin himself to flee France, were being imprisoned and even executed on the charge that they were endangering the welfare of the nation and were guilty of sedition.

The excellence of this work, as a theological statement, however, was such that it soon enjoyed wide-spread popularity. This reception, of course, increased its demand and served as an incentive, among others, for Calvin to produce further editions. The second edition appeared in 1539 at Strasbourg and reflects the fact that he had indeed become aware of his wide-spread audience. Although in this and subsequent editions the apologetic elements were retained, the development and addition of materials show that Calvin's aim was increasingly one of instruction, whether of pastors and theological students or the general public.

A third edition appeared at Strasbourg in 1543 with substantial additions. It was reissued in 1545. The fifth edition, published at Geneva in 1550, is the next major expansion. This edition was republished in 1553 and 1554.

The eighth and definitive edition appeared at Geneva in 1559. This is the edition upon which the English translations of Thomas Norton (1523-1584), John Allen (1771-1839), and Henry Beveridge (1799-1863), as well as the recent translation of Ford Battles, are all based. It is slightly over five times the size of the 1536 and 1553 editions. Thus the 1559 edition both reflects a rather thorough reworking of Calvin's ideas and, as well, furnishes us with a comprehensive statement of what those ideas were not too long prior to his death in 1564.

1. The 1559 Edition

The material in this edition with which we will be most directly concerned is the exposition of the fourth commandment in Book 2, Chapter 8, "Explanation of the Moral Law (the ten commandments)."[15] Section 28 begins with a statement of basic intention: "The purpose of this commandment is that, being dead to our own inclinations and works, we should meditate on the Kingdom of God, and that we should practice that meditation in the ways established by him." [394] At the outset, then, Calvin introduces the idea that at the heart of the teaching of this commandment is the conflict between spiritual meditation and our own inclinations and works. This is a key notion that needs careful appraisal. Exactly what it means will become more apparent as our discussion unfolds. It is an idea that will be encountered repeatedly, one, as will be seen, that has far-reaching consequences for the whole of Calvin's view.

Having made this general opening statement, Calvin next observes that this commandment requires a different kind ("seriem"[16]) of exposition, "since (it) has a peculiar consideration distinct from the others." [394] He credits the early church fathers with having partially understood this fact, since many of them, recognizing a typical element not found in the other nine commandments, namely, the keeping of a day, concluded that this commandment was abolished along with other figures at the coming of Christ. "This they say truly, but they touch upon only half the matter." [395] The exposition of this commandment must go much deeper and its keeping consists in meeting three basic requirements:

> First, under the repose of the seventh day the heavenly Lawgiver meant to represent to the people of Israel spiritual rest, in which believers ought to lay aside their own works to allow God to work in them. Secondly, he meant that there was to be a stated day for them to assemble to hear the law and perform the rites, or at least to devote it particularly to meditation upon his works, and thus through this remembrance to be trained in piety. Thirdly, he resolved to give a day of rest to servants and those who are under the authority of others, in order that they should have some respite from toil. [395]

These three considerations, in the above order, largely occupy Calvin in the remainder of his exposition.

"Nevertheless we are taught in many passages that this foreshadowing of spiritual rest [spiritualis quietis adumbrationem] occupied the chief place in the Sabbath." [395] So Calvin begins section 29. He then dwells at some length on the importance and stress put on this commandment in the Old Testament. Obedience to no other commandment is more strictly enforced. The slightest infraction demands capital punishment (Exod. 31:14; Num. 15:32-36).[17] Violation of the Sabbath is often used as a synecdoche to express the fact that all religion has been subverted (Ezek. 20:12-13; Isa. 56:1-2). The giving of the Sabbath is considered to be an high point in God's revelation to Israel (Neh. 9:14).

When, however, these verses and others like them are taken as a whole, the uniform teaching of the Old Testament is this: the Sabbath was given to Israel as a promissory sign that God would be their sanctifier (Exod. 31:13; Ezek. 20:12). Thus, the emphasis again falls on the principle with which, we have already seen, Calvin begins his exposition: the fourth commandment is basically concerned with the conflict between true spirituality and our own sinful thoughts, words, and deeds.

Nowhere in all the material subsequently to be examined does Calvin give clearer expression to that principle than here.[18] The "inward reality" [re ipsa interiori], corresponding to the "outward sign" [signi externi] given to Israel, is that, "We must be wholly at rest that God may work in us; we must yield our will; we must resign our heart; we must give up all our fleshly desires. In short, we must rest from all activities of our own contriving so that, having God working in us, we may repose in him (Heb. 4:9), as the apostle also teaches." [396] To summarize and at the same time anticipate one of the most basic conclusions of our study, for Calvin the Sabbath rest consists in cessation on the part of God's people from works done under the impulses of sin, so that God may accomplish within them his work of sanctification.

The next problem of immediate concern to Calvin is the significance of the appointment of one day in seven as the day of rest. He begins section 30 with a particularly interesting statement. "For the Jews the observance of one day in seven customarily represented this eternal cessation [perpetuam istam cessationem]." [396] Almost casually, as it seems, further light is shed on what he means by cessation from sin, which, as already noted above, he considers to be a basic element in the requirement of this commandment. It is "eternal cessation." Ultimately, then, the injunction to rest on one day in seven is not only a command to cease from sin in this life, but as well anticipates the eternal state of the redeemed when they shall be free from sin.

The main reason why the Jews rested on the seventh day was that on that day God himself rested. "The Lord commended it by his own example that they might observe it with greater piety." [396] And Calvin goes on to add that there is no greater incentive for obeying this commandment than the fact that in keeping it, the creature is imitating the Creator.

It is difficult to see how those who have asserted either that Calvin nowhere teaches that the Sabbath is grounded in creation or, specifically, that this idea is missing in the *Institutes*,[19] could have overlooked the import of this statement. Certainly there is no explicit mention, in terms of language that came into vogue in later discussions, that the Sabbath is a "creation ordinance"; nor does he say that it was observed prior to the giving of the Law at Sinai. But it is equally certain that he here refers implicitly to the teaching of Genesis 2:2-3, and that the rest of God described in these verses furnishes a basis, if not the basis, for the Sabbath command given to Israel. Admittedly we might wish that he had been more explicit, but we should hardly expect a statement in terms of language which was largely determined by the long and intense debates that did not begin until after Calvin's death. In short, the notion of the Sabbath institution as a creation ordinance (in the sense of being grounded in God's own resting after creating), although not explicitly stated, is consonant with and perhaps even implied in the teaching of the *Institutes*.

Why specifically did God single out the seventh day as the day of rest? For those who would seek "some secret meaning in the number seven," [396] Calvin gives the following suggestions. There are two possible interpretations. Both are based on the fact that in Scripture the number seven is the number of perfection. First, it appropriately indicates perpetuity. This is confirmed by the language of Moses in Genesis 2:3 where the seventh day is the day of perpetual, eternal rest from the work of creation. Here Calvin explicitly refers to the words of Moses, "as he relates, 'the Lord rested from his work,'" indicating again, at the very least, that in his mind there is a definite relation between the fourth commandment and the rest of God from the work of creation.

Secondly, the number seven indicates that the Sabbath will not be perfected until the eschatological Last Day.

For we here begin our blessed rest in him; daily we make fresh progress in it. But because there is still a continual warfare with the flesh, it will not be consummated until Isaiah's saying is fulfilled about "new moon following new moon and Sabbath following

Sabbath" (Isa. 66:23); until, that is, God shall be "all in all" (1 Cor. 15:28). [396]

By setting aside each seventh day, God provided a picture of the great and final Sabbath for his people and thus encouraged them to aspire to and meditate upon its perfection.

Two points are worth underscoring in connection with Calvin's development of this second interpretation. First, he again makes the characteristic point that Sabbath rest is to be contrasted with sinful works, and that such rest will ultimately be realized only when our "continual warfare with sinful flesh" is over. Second, it is clear that whatever else the significance of the weekly day of rest given to the Jews, its reference is eschatological. It looks beyond the advent of Christ to the consummation for its ultimate realization and fulfillment. It is particularly important to take note of this second point, for as we shall have occasion to see later, on it Calvin apparently contradicts himself.

It is difficult to tell from his discussion just what Calvin considers the significance of the number seven to be, whether he favors either one of the suggestions offered or considers them both to be equally probable. Whatever the answer may be, the demand for a solution to this problem largely diminishes when Calvin begins the next section (31) by saying that if anyone thinks his interpretation of the number seven is "too subtle," he is perfectly content that it be understood "more simply."

He then proceeds to state what is obviously a minimal expression of what is acceptable to him in this matter, and in so doing provides what he considers to be the essence of the Sabbath commandment given to Israel. He is content if all accept that

the Lord ordained a certain day on which his people might, under the tutelage of the law, practice constant meditation upon the spiritual rest. And he assigned the seventh day, either because he foresaw that it would be sufficient; or that, by providing a model in his own example, he might better arouse the people; or at least point out to them that the Sabbath had no other purpose than to render them conformable to their Creator's example. Which interpretation we accept makes little difference, provided we retain the mystery [mysteriam] that is principally set forth: that of perpetual repose from our labors [de perpetua nostrorum operum quiete]. [397]

This statement makes clear that Calvin does not consider the appointment of the seventh day specifically, to be the day of rest, as important in itself. The day God chose is a matter of indifference. The most that can be said is that in choosing the day on which he himself rested he provides an added incentive for us to keep that day, or that it reminds us of the general principle that the goal of the creature is conformity to his Creator. But those things are still really incidental to the teaching of the fourth commandment. The point of fundamental importance is that the Sabbath ordinance given to Israel presented the "mystery," the foreshadowing of "perpetual repose from labors." It does not appear to be a misrepresentation of Calvin's position to say that regardless of what day of the week God would have chosen for Israel's Sabbath, the essence of the fourth commandment would be the same: a promise and foretaste of spiritual rest and a challenge to meditate upon that promise.

Here again the emphasis falls on what we have already seen is a basic motif of the fourth commandment for Calvin: the contrast between sinful works and spiritual rest in God. He adds, "The prophets repeatedly recalled the Jews to the consideration of this [i.e., spiritual rest] in order that they might not think they had performed their whole duty merely by ceasing from physical labor." [397] He then cites Isaiah 58:13-14 as an example. Clearly, then, Calvin recognized that keeping the fourth commandment under the Old Testament economy consisted in more than mere physical inactivity.

His concluding comments on the first reason why the Sabbath was given to Israel confront us with a statement of admitted difficulty.

But there is no doubt that by the Lord Christ's coming the ceremonial part of this commandment was abolished [Caeterum non dubium quin Domini Christi adventu, quod ceremoniale hic erat, abolitum fuerit]. For he himself is the truth, with whose presence all figures vanish; he is the body, at whose appearance the shadows are left behind. He is, I say, the true fulfillment [complementum] of the Sabbath. [397]

Not too surprisingly, this statement and others like it have been in the spotlight in subsequent controversies about the Sabbath. Unfortunately, too often they have been misread or misrepresented, and implications drawn from them that are hardly justified. Not infrequently they have been wrenched out of context and made to do service for views they were never intended to support. Those who seek to show that the Lord's Day is not commanded in the Decalogue or is only faintly analogous to the Sabbath are particularly guilty of this charge. Little effort has been put into finding out what Calvin had in mind when he says, "the ceremonial part of this commandment was abolished."

What does this statement mean? Posing that question with an eye to the immediate context enables us to draw certain conclusions with confidence. The "ceremonial part" of the commandment is what Calvin previously called a "mystery," a "figure," or a "foreshadowing" of spiritual rest. Further, that typical element has found its full reality in the coming of the Messiah. The promise of rest from sin has been completely fulfilled by the advent of Christ.

The remarks directly following the statement in question confirm these conclusions. In support of his view that the ceremonial element is abrogated, Calvin quotes two passages. Colossians 2:16-17, he believes, clearly shows the promissory element in the fourth commandment to be included within that body of Old Testament typology that finds its antitype, its substance, in the earthly ministry of Christ.

Romans 6:4 ff. sheds more light for Calvin on the spiritual

rest promised in the fourth commandment. First, the sinner, through the exercise of faith and repentance, has property in the death and resurrection of Christ and so may walk in "newness of life." This "newness of life" presently enjoyed by the believer Calvin equates, it appears, with the spiritual rest promised to Israel in the Sabbath institution.

Second, the wider context of Paul's teaching in Romans 6 and 7 underscores for Calvin the close association between the fourth commandment and the doctrine of sanctification as a whole. He has already stated (in section 29), as we have seen, that the Sabbath was a sign to Israel that God would be their sanctifier. Here he adds that this "newness of life" (Rom. 6:4-5), the substance of the truth of the fourth commandment, "is not confined within a single day but extends through the whole course of our life, until, completely dead to ourselves, we are filled with the life of God. Christians ought therefore to shun completely the superstitious observance of days." [397]

Before leaving Calvin's discussion of his first main point, two questions need to be raised. The first concerns the statement just quoted. What does he have in mind when he speaks of the "superstitious observance of days"? Surely the practices of the medieval church are in view.[20] But does he perhaps also include the observance commanded of Old Testament Israel? That question has been widely debated. How it is to be answered can only be discussed fully later, when more data has been introduced, but for the present we may note that Calvin has already pointed out that even for the Jews the Sabbath institution was never intended merely as a command to physical inactivity but also involved meditation upon the religious significance of that rest.

A second question concerns what may appear to be a self-contradiction. Section 30, as we have seen, is clear in stating that the weekly day for rest given to Israel is a figure that will not be ultimately realized until the eschatological Last Day. The quotations just examined, however, are equally clear in maintaining that Christ, in his first coming, is the "true fulfillment of the Sabbath." It might seem, then, that Calvin is inconsistent, or at least not clear, in setting forth what he himself considers to be the basic teaching of the commandment.

A writer of Calvin's acuity would not likely overlook a conflict between two statements in such close proximity to each other. The likely solution lies in recognizing that for him "newness of life," the actual possession of God's people after Christ's first coming, is virtually identical with the final rest to be ushered in at the Last Day. We will have occasion to evaluate the accuracy of this conclusion later.

To summarize our findings to this point, the primary reason in God's giving the Sabbath to the Jews was, by means of that weekly day of rest, to promise spiritual rest from sin. That promise was fulfilled at the first coming of Christ, who has made the believer to enjoy the reality of the promised rest on every day. The typical function of the Sabbath, then, as a foreshadowing of spiritual rest on the seventh day, or any other day of the week, has ceased to exist. In that sense the Sabbath may be said to have been abolished. Although he does not consider it basic to the meaning of this commandment, the reason for singling out the seventh day as the day of rest was to remind Israel of the perfect rest enjoyed by God on that day and so encourage their desire to share in it.

The Sabbath no longer serves as a type. But, as he goes on in section 32, Calvin would not have us conclude that the other two reasons for giving the Sabbath to Israel have similarly ceased to be in force. On the contrary, they apply equally to all people in every age. "Although the Sabbath has been abrogated, there is still occasion for us: (1) to assemble on stated days for the hearing of the Word, the breaking of the mystical bread, and for public prayers; (2) to give surcease from labor to servants and workmen. There is no doubt that in enjoining the Sabbath the Lord was concerned with both." [398][21]

The Scriptural basis for the latter of these two reasons is straight forward and presents no problems. Calvin quotes the relevant part of the fourth commandment itself, as given in

Deuteronomy (5:14-15), and its partial statement in Exodus 23:12.

However, his basis for establishing public worship as a requirement of the fourth commandment is not so clear. He makes no appeal to the language of the commandment itself and refers to other Scriptures only indirectly. His argument may be summarized as follows: The New Testament gives abundant evidence that the church gathered for public meetings. Moreover, from our own experience we know how much we need such worship. At this point, however, a practical problem arises. "But how can such meetings be held unless they have been established and have their stated days [suos constitutos dies]?" [398] Here Calvin appeals to the principle governing the assembling of the church in 1 Corinthians 14:40 ("all things should be done decently and in order"). For such decency and order to be maintained rules and regulations governing worship are absolutely indispensable, otherwise the church will deteriorate into confusion and chaos. So he concludes, "But if we are subject to the same necessity as that to alleviate which the Lord established the Sabbath for the Jews, let no one allege that this has nothing to do with us."

It is clear, particularly from the last quotation, that Calvin is concerned to ground the present obligation for public worship in the fourth commandment.[22] It may be asked, however, whether, even in Calvin's own mind, his appeal is not rather substantially to the principle of decency and order or to some other consideration not specifically mentioned, than to the Sabbath institution. Raising this question in a sense anticipates evaluation of Calvin but is necessary here in order to achieve a clear picture of his position.

The relevance of this question is underscored by certain remarks Calvin makes by way of anticipating an objection from his readers. In reply to anyone who might ask why the church does not do away with "all distinction of days" and gather for worship every day, Calvin replies that he only wishes that such a situation could be a reality. "Spiritual wisdom truly deserved to have some portion of time set apart for it each day. "But," he continues, "if the weakness of many made it impossible for daily meetings to be held, and the rule of love does not allow more to be required of them, why should we not obey the order [rationi] we see laid upon us by God's will?" [398]

The substance of Calvin's argument is along the following lines. The ideal set before the church is that it gather daily for public worship. The weakness and spiritual immaturity of many of its members, however, makes realizing that ideal impossible. Therefore, balancing these two factors, to set aside one day each week for public assembly makes provision for a partial realization of the ideal, of which all are capable.

There are certain difficulties in Calvin's language on this point that may not be overlooked. First is what can hardly be described as anything other than an air of accommodation and expediency in his appeal to the fourth commandment. To paraphrase him, "The ideal for Christians is to gather daily for worship but since this ideal is not practically realizable, let us, on the basis of the fourth commandment, set aside one day each week for public assembly." To say the least, this constitutes a rather negative and oblique appeal to the authority of one of the ten commandments. It is particularly strange in Calvin's case, for, as we shall see below, he holds the highest possible estimation of the Decalogue.[23]

A second problem arises with Calvin's appeal to the principle, already cited, that a portion of each day should be set aside for public worship. The propriety of such a rule is not at issue here. Rather, the difficulty lies in seeing how it is even remotely relevant to the teaching of the fourth commandment, much less demanded by it. Likely Calvin viewed spiritual rest and public worship as so intimately associated, that to affirm the perpetual character of the former is to imply the daily propriety of the latter. For him, the highest and most appropriate expression of spiritual resting is worship.

Although at this point he has finished his formal exposition of the fourth commandment, Calvin feels "compelled to dwell longer on this because at present some restless spirits are stirring up tumult over the Lord's Day." [398[24]] What exactly was the charge of these "restless spirits"? "They complain that Christian people are nourished in Judaism because they keep some observance of days." [399] In replying to this allegation (section 33), Calvin deals at some length with the basis for Sunday as the Christian day of worship.

Before considering that discussion any further, however, a parenthetical observation is in order. From both the last quotation and the incident mentioned in the preceding footnote, the "restless spirits" in view are clearly Anabaptists, or at least, have Anabaptist leanings. In short, section 33 offers the strongest possible evidence against the view that in the *Institutes*, Calvin's apologetic efforts are directed solely against Roman Catholic viewpoints.[25]

In reply to the charge that the Christian celebration of Sunday is a remnant of Judaism, Calvin argues that there is a basic difference between the Jewish Sabbath and the Christian Sunday. "For we are not celebrating it as a ceremony with the most rigid scrupulousness, supposing a spiritual mystery to be figured thereby. Rather, we are using it as a remedy [remedium] needed to keep order in the church." [399] It should be noted how here again Calvin emphasizes, perhaps more pointedly than earlier, that the observance of Sunday as the day of worship is based on decidedly negative considerations. The authority of the fourth commandment that obtains in this case serves as a "remedy."

When objections are raised to this view, on the basis of Scriptures that flatly prohibit the observation of days by Christians,[26] Calvin is quick to add that only "madmen" [furiosos] can fail to see the kind of observance Paul has in view. The "distinction of days" the apostle speaks out against is not setting aside one day each week for worship out of a concern for church order, but the retention of the Sabbath as though it still typified something spiritual for Christians. People who thus continued to maintain the Old Testament Sabbath, Calvin continues, kept the day of rest not because it gave them time for meditation, but because "they imagined that by celebrating the day they were honoring mysteries once commended." [399]

Consequently, they obscured the coming of Christ and his work as the fulfillment of Old Testament promise. Such people were guilty of a truly "superstitious observance of days." "The apostle inveighs, I say, against this absurd distinction of days, not against the lawful selection that serves the peace of the Christian fellowship." He then cites the command to the Corinthians (1 Cor. 16:2) that they meet on the first day of the week to gather contributions for the Jerusalem church, as proof that Paul himself recognized a certain distinction of days. "[T]he Sabbath was retained" for this and similar purposes, he says, showing again that he plainly considers concern for church order to be prescribed by the fourth commandment.

In bringing his discussion of Sunday observance to a close, Calvin reminds the "restless spirits" that their fears of Jewish superstition are not the only concern in evaluating the Christian observance of Sunday. Such superstition is always a danger, he grants, although much less so in the case of the Lord's Day than for the Sabbaths the Jews used to keep. But the necessity for setting aside a weekly day of worship must also be a recognized. "For, because it was expedient to overthrow superstition, the day sacred to the Jews was set aside; because it was necessary to maintain decorum, order, and peace in the church, another was appointed for that purpose." [399]

This statement explicitly mentions the appointment of the Lord's Day in place of the Jewish Sabbath. That brings into view another question intensely debated subsequent to Calvin's day. On what basis and by whom was the Lord's Day instituted? By whose authority did Sunday become the Christian day of rest and/or public worship?

Our earlier caution applies here as well. An answer to these questions in language and formulations from after Calvin's time should not be expected. In fact, he has very little to say about this issue, and what he does say is not always easy to understand exactly.

Section 34, the last in his exposition of the fourth commandment, begins with this observation: "However, the ancients did not substitute the Lord's Day (as we call it) for the Sabbath without careful discrimination." [399] This is the second time in his exposition that the "ancients" are mentioned. In section 28, as we saw, the "early fathers"[27] are commended for perceiving that the typical character of the Sabbath has been abolished. Who specifically or even what era of the church's history Calvin has in mind is difficult to say. Because these references are so vague, they likely have in view those who held authority in the church in its very earliest days, those under whose direction Sunday was first set aside as the Christian day of rest and public worship.

At any rate, Calvin plainly credits these "ancients" with having substituted the Lord's Day for the Sabbath. That substitution, out of concern for the welfare of the church, was not made more or less arbitrarily. The "ancients," he goes on to point out, saw a definite relationship between the Old Testament Sabbath and the Lord's Day. With "careful discrimination" they chose the first day of the week in place of the seventh, because on it Christ's resurrection occurred, an event that brought an end to all types and ushered in the rest foreshadowed in the Old Testament Sabbath.

Not only does Calvin not say that the "ancients" made the change of day arbitrarily, but also neither does he say the change was made solely on the basis of their own authority. Whether or not they were given special revelation no longer available to us is a question he simply does not consider. That one of these two alternatives is more probably in his mind can neither be affirmed nor denied solely on the basis of the statement just quoted.

However, the supposition that he views the change of day as being made without express divine authorization finds strong support in what he has to say shortly after his statement about the "ancients" making that change.

Nor do I cling to the number "seven" so as to bind the church in subjection to it. And I shall not condemn churches that have other solemn days for their meetings, provided there be no superstition. This will be so if they have regard solely to the maintenance of discipline and good order. [400]

Perhaps more than any other, this passage, particularly the first two sentences, has been torn from its context to show how lax Calvin's views on the Sabbath question were. But even when it is taken in context, he is hardly holding that the change of day was sanctioned by divine authority. One moment he asserts that the shift from the seventh to the first stemmed from recognizing the intrinsic significance of Christ's resurrection, after "careful discrimination." In the next breath virtually, he informs the reader that he has little concern which day of the week is chosen for public assembly, as long as discipline and order are maintained.

Consequently, we should recognize, Calvin did not hold that the change from the seventh to the first day ultimately rests on special revelation. He would hardly have regarded a divine ordinance with such carelessness and indifference. On the other hand, neither should we suppose that for him the time and frequency of Christian public worship bear little or no relation to the fourth commandment. As we shall see presently, he held the most emphatic and uncompromising views on the perpetual validity and obligation of the Decalogue. And, to note the obvious, all that we have so far been considering comes from his exposition of the fourth element in the Decalogue, what is demanded and taught by it.

The likely proper conclusion, then, is that Calvin considers the specific day on which Christians assemble for worship a matter not integral to God's command. Therefore, the action of the "ancients" in substituting the first day for the seventh, although personally acceptable to him, was solely their own and not based on revelation.

In drawing his exposition to a close, Calvin gives his own summary, worth quoting in its entirety, of what the fourth commandment means for believers today.

To sum up: as truth was delivered to the Jews under a figure, so is it set before us without shadows. First, we are to meditate throughout life upon an everlasting Sabbath rest from all our works, that the Lord may work in us through his Spirit. Secondly, each one of us privately, whenever he has leisure, is to exercise himself diligently in pious meditation upon God's work. Also, we should all observe together the lawful order set by the church for the hearing of the Word, the administration of the sacraments, and for public prayers. In the third place, we should not inhumanly oppress those subject to us. [400]

Most of what is said here has already been discussed at length. Two ideas, however, appear that have been no more than mentioned previously (in section 28): the injunction for private meditation and the prohibition of the oppression of laborers, servants and the like by their employers and masters. These notions will be encountered again below and discussed further then.

Calvin does not conclude, however, before turning his attention to another erroneous point of view. If the summary just given is carefully heeded, then, he maintains, will "vanish the trifles of the false prophets, who in former centuries infected the people with a Jewish opinion." [400] What exactly was this "Jewish opinion"? "They asserted that nothing but the ceremonial part of this commandment has been abrogated (in their phraseology the 'appointing'[28] of the seventh day), but the moral part remains – namely, the fixing of one day in seven."

To find in these words a condemnation of the view later set forth, for instance, in the *Westminster Confession of Faith*, chapter 21, section 7 is without the slightest grounds. Calvin does not tell us who these "false prophets" were, but in a footnote (43) McNeill cites certain materials of Albertus Magnus and Aquinas that reflect the opinion Calvin is condemning.

At any rate, Calvin almost certainly has in mind the general attitude toward the Sabbath that developed during the medieval period. On that view, as we have seen in chapter 1, there is identity between Jewish Sabbath and Christian Lord's Day, except that each is observed on a different day; the rationale for and obligations of the Jewish Saturday carry over to the Christian Sunday. And this, Calvin holds, is nothing less than changing the day out of contempt for the Jews, while retaining the same sanctity of the day and the same typical foreshadowing that pertained to the Jews. Further, as he surveys existing conditions in the Roman Catholic Church, he can only conclude that the teaching of these "false prophets" has resulted in what might be expected. "For those of them who cling to their constitutions surpass the Jews three times over in crass and carnal Sabbatarian [sabbathismi] superstition." [400] To them, Calvin says, apply equally the warnings of Isaiah rebuking the children of Israel (1:13-15; 58:13). [401] Whatever the merits of the moral-ceremonial distinction drawn by the Westminster Confession, it is not the view of the "false prophets" Calvin condemns.[29]

A matter already noted is worth underscoring at this point. Twice Calvin departs from the narrow course of exposition to deal with views he deems false, the positions first of the "restless spirits" and then of the "false prophets." Each is the polar opposite of the other on the Sabbath question. The "false prophets," reflecting a Roman Catholic viewpoint, held that the Lord's Day is a strict continuation of the Jewish Sabbath. The "restless spirits," representing an Anabaptist outlook, opposed any distinction of days. This shows that Calvin's exposition has the widest possible apologetic interest and represents a correspondingly comprehensive statement of his views. There is no warrant for concluding that he limits himself exclusively or even predominately to any one particular front or group of readers.

The final sentence of the entire exposition seems intended to state, in kernel form, what Calvin considers the most important single practical element in the teaching of the fourth commandment, what above all else this commandment requires of the church today. "But we ought especially to hold to this general doctrine: that, in order to prevent religion from either perishing or declining among us, we should diligently frequent the sacred meetings, and make use of those external aids which can promote the worship of God." [401] What has been indicated throughout by the tenor of the discussion as a whole is expressly affirmed here. For Calvin the preeminent practical concern of the fourth commandment is the maintenance of public worship.

Calvin and the Decalogue

In the interests of achieving fuller clarity on Calvin's Sabbath views, we ought to consider, if only briefly, his view of the ten commandments as a unit, taken as a whole.[30]

In the final analysis, the ten commandments are a more extensive publication of the demands of the moral law, demands that may be defined more basically under two heads, the obligations to love God and to love neighbor as self.

This identity between the Decalogue and moral law is apparent from several angles. First, the exposition of each of the commandments, in sequence, comprises the substance of Book 2, Chapter 8, with the title, "Explanation of the Moral Law" [Legis moralis explicatio].[31] Revealing as this title and arrangement may be, we are not without the most explicit statement on the identity of moral law and ten commandments. In an early section (12) of the chapter, in discussing certain matters preparatory to his exposition of each commandment, the opening sentences read:

> The whole law is contained under two heads. Yet our God, to remove all possibility of excuse, willed to set forth more fully and clearly by the ten commandments everything connected with the honor, fear, and love of him, and everything pertaining to the love toward men, which he for his own sake enjoins upon us. [377]

The ten commandments, then, are a fuller setting forth of the moral law, as scanning the structure and contents of this chapter easily verifies.

At this point the question might be posed: Could it be that Calvin held that the ten commandments are to be identified with the moral law, but only in the sense that they are a publication of it given specifically to Israel, whose validity ceased when the theocracy ended?

Calvin certainly gives no indication that he holds any such notion. In the passage just quoted, he states unequivocally that the ten commandments require of us everything connected with love of God and others. Moreover, earlier, in chapter 7, section 13, he deals particularly with those who declare that the validity of the ten commandments has ceased. "Certain ignorant persons, . . .rashly cast out the whole of Moses, and bid farewell to the two Tables of the Law." [361] After admonishing those who hold "this wicked thought," Calvin draws his conclusion,

> But if no one can deny that a perfect pattern of righteousness stands forth in the law,[32] either we need no rule to live rightly and justly, or it is forbidden to depart from the law. There are not many rules, but one everlasting and unchangeable rule to live by. For this reason we are not to refer solely to one age David's statement that the life of a righteous man is a continual meditation upon the law (Ps. 1:2), for it is just as applicable to every age, even to the end of the world. [362]

The two tables of the law, that is, the ten commandments, as a statement of the moral law, apply "to every age, even to the end of the world."

At the risk of being repetitious, but so that there might be no uncertainty on this point, is the following statement from a different context .

> The moral law ... is contained under two heads, one of which simply commands us to worship God with pure faith and piety; the other, to embrace men with sincere affection. Accordingly, it is the true and eternal rule of righteousness, prescribed for men of all nations and times, who wish to conform their lives to God's will. For it is his eternal and unchangeable will that he himself indeed be worshiped by us all, and that we love one another.[33]

The point to be drawn from Calvin's view of the Decalogue pertinent to our study is this: any remarks he makes regarding the meaning and present obligation of the Sabbath can be understood and properly evaluated only within the scope of his firm conviction that the fourth commandment, as an element of the Decalogue, applies to all people in every age. There is not the slightest indication that he had the remotest sympathy for the view, though subsequently it has often appealed to him in support, that the Sabbath no longer exists, on the basis either that the Decalogue is not valid for the Christian era or that the fourth commandment alone has been abolished while the other nine are still in force.[34] Rather, he plainly opposes any view of the Sabbath question based on the notion of the abrogation of all or even one of the ten commandments.

Therefore, when Calvin expresses himself to the effect that the Sabbath has been abrogated or that it is a matter of indifference on which day of the week Christians gather for worship, such statements are subject to qualification and have their sense in light of his more basic, controlling conviction that the fourth commandment is valid, as he says, "even to the end of the world."

Summary
The important features of the teaching of the 1559 edition of the *Institutes* may be summarized in the following propositions.

1. The weekly day of rest which Israel was ordered to keep by the fourth commandment fulfilled three distinct functions.

   a) It was a promissory sign, typical of the spiritual rest from sin which God would one day give to his people. For Israel to keep the Sabbath rest was in effect to confess that God was its sanctifier (Ezek. 20:12).

   b) It provided a day for public assembly, a stated time for hearing the law and offering sacrifices.

   c) It provided a day of rest from toil for slaves and servants.

2. At the first advent of Christ, culminating in his death and resurrection, the Sabbath ceased to function as a type. The spiritual rest promised to Israel by the weekly day of rest, has become a full reality. Christians now enjoy that rest on every day of their lives. In this sense, as a type of spiritual rest, the Sabbath has been abrogated and should no longer be observed.

3. Although the typical character of the Sabbath no longer exists, the other two functions of the Sabbath given to Israel are still in force.

a) The fourth commandment requires the public assembly of the church at stated times for the use of the word, sacraments, and prayer. Maintenance of public worship is an important specific concern of this commandment. Which day of the week is set aside for this assembly, whether one or more, is a matter of indifference.

b) The fourth commandment requires that rest be given to those who in their labors are subject to the authority of others.

4. The fourth commandment must always be seen in its context, that is, as part of the Decalogue, which applies to all people in every age.

2. The 1536 Edition

This edition of the *Institutes* appeared at Basel, where Calvin had fled persecution begun by Francis I. It provides a defense of the position held by those who were being persecuted and represents Calvin's first work of importance. As in the 1559 edition, the material to be dealt with comprises an exposition of the fourth commandment. It is part of the first chapter, "The Law: Containing an Explanation of the Decalogue."[35]

What we have seen to be true in the definitive edition applies here as well. As the chapter title itself reflects, the Law of God, which has abiding validity, is identified with the Decalogue. Here, too, our discussion must be governed by Calvin's underlying conviction that the fourth commandment holds for all people at all times.

The length of the exposition is roughly two-thirds of that of the 1559 edition. The thrust is basically the same, though with certain differences in emphasis. Observing the Sabbath, he begins, pertains "both to piety and to the worship of God" [23], since the fourth commandment is contained in the first table of the law – a thought implied throughout the 1559 edition but never explicitly stated. He then goes on to discuss, in virtually the same terms as in 1559, the high regard with which the Sabbath was held throughout the Old Testament era. Sabbath desecration is used by the prophets as a synecdoche to indicate that all religion has been polluted. There is no commandment that the Lord more strictly enforces.

The distinctive element in this commandment is that it is "shadowy" [umbratile]. It was commanded of Israel during the period of ceremonies to teach them by the "outward" [externa] observance of a day of rest the nature of spiritual rest and service. "But there is absolutely no doubt that this precept was a foreshadowing, and enjoined upon the Jews during the era of ceremonies, in order to represent to them under outward observance the spiritual worship of God." [23]

At the coming of Christ, however, this commandment was abrogated along with all the other types of the Old Testament economy. "Therefore, at the coming of Christ, who is the light of shadows and the truth of the figures, it was abolished, like the remaining shadows of the Mosaic law, ..." [23] Galatians 4 and Colossians 3 are cited as clear proof.[36] This rather sweeping statement, however, is immediately qualified. The ceremonial character of the Sabbath, specifically, what served a tutelary function for Israel, has been abolished. The "truth" of the commandment is abiding and applies to all. "But, though the ceremonies [caeremonia, sing.] and outward rite have been abolished, ... we still retain the truth of the precept, that the Lord willed the Jews and us to have forever and in common." [23][37]

What is this truth? First, that we should enter into the spiritual rest provided by Christ. That means that we must cease from our own sinful works and rest in God, letting him, by the Holy Spirit, work in us. To submit to the dominion of the Holy Spirit is to obey the fourth commandment. "All works of this sort are servile. From them the law of the Sabbath bids us cease, that God may dwell in us, may effect what is good, and rule us by the leading of his Holy Spirit, whose kingdom imparts peace and tranquility to the conscience." [23]

This is the same initial emphasis as in the 1559 edition. The Sabbath instituted for Israel, the rest of every seventh day, was set entirely within a redemptive context. It was a promissory sign of the spiritual rest and peace from sin the Messiah would secure for his people. At the coming of Christ that spiritual rest became a full reality and, consequently, the weekly Sabbath ceased, at that time, to have a typical function.

In developing these ideas, Calvin is more positive than in the 1559 edition. Here his emphasis is not so much on the abolition of the type as on the meaning of its realization. The idea of sanctification is clearly stated, and the agency of the Holy Spirit in bringing spiritual rest is expressly mentioned.

On the question of the significance of the seventh day, Calvin is also more positive than in the 1559 edition. His position is the same in both, but here he gives no indication that he is willing to compromise this conviction for those who find his interpretation "too subtle."[38]

The number seven in Scripture is the number of perfection; it signifies perpetuity. The appointment of the seventh day as Israel's Sabbath, therefore, serves two functions. First, it teaches that in giving a weekly day of rest, God promised his people a perpetual Sabbath, one that is without end. Indeed, God's Sabbath will not be perfectly fulfilled or kept until the great, eschatological Last Day. The Christian has the privilege even now to enter partially into that eternal rest, but must strive to make daily progress in the enjoyment of it until the time it will be perfectly realized. The believer's present rest in Christ may never be dissociated from the eternal rest in heaven. "For we have now begun through faith our rest in God, in which we are also daily making progress so that at least [sic [39]] it may be completed when that saying of Isaiah will be fulfilled, in which Sabbath upon Sabbath is promised to God's church (Isa. 66:23). That is, when God will be all in all (I Cor. 15:28)." [23-24].

The second reason for appointing the seventh day is to remind that it was on this day that God himself rested from his work of creation. It is of the greatest advantage to the creature to know that he can pattern his life after the Creator, that if he rests from his works as God did from his, he will experience that perfect rest that God himself enjoys. "This also God [Dominus] showed us in the creation of the world, which he completed in six days; only on the seventh day did he rest from all work [opere], so that by his example we also, ceasing from our labors [operibus], may seek our rest in him, and aspire eagerly[40] to this sabbath of the seventh day." [24]

This reference to the rest of God from creation again underlines that for Calvin a definite relationship exists between the Sabbath institution and divine rest. To be sure, as we noted in discussing the 1559 edition, there is no explicit mention of a creation ordinance. Nor does he say that the Sabbath was kept before the giving of the law at Sinai.

On the other hand, there is not the slightest ground, no more here than in the definitive edition, for the view that the fourth commandment was for Israel and Israel alone, or that the language of the commandment referring to hallowing the seventh day at creation is merely proleptic. Rather, Calvin is quite clear that God's rest at creation is an example and norm for "us," including the New Testament Christian. Moreover, Calvin's view of the Decalogue is pertinent here. The fourth commandment, as well as the other nine, has nothing less than a universal and abiding validity. The notion of the Sabbath as a creation ordinance, then, although not expressly stated, is certainly consonant with his teaching in this edition. This entire question – the origin of the Sabbath – will be discussed further when we examine his comments on Genesis 2:3.

The same dissonance noted in the 1559 edition is also present here. On the one hand, the spiritual rest foreshadowed under Israel's Sabbath has been realized at the first advent of Christ – so much so that the Sabbath as a promissory sign of that rest has been abolished; the figure has been replaced by the reality. On the other hand, that spiritual rest, he asserts with comparable, if not equal, force, will not be fully realized until the great, eschatological Last Day.

To find a basic self-contradiction here is neither necessary or, given Calvin's customary incisiveness, plausible. Rather, as suggested earlier, the solution lies in recognizing that he virtually equates spiritual rest actually enjoyed by believers since the coming of Christ with eternal rest, so that the distinction between present rest and final rest is only one of degree.

The Lord's Day, he continues, is related to the Sabbath. It has not been instituted, however, for Christians to keep, as if it had some sacredness of itself or retains the typical significance that characterized the Old Testament Sabbath. "This applies to the Lord's Day which we now observe: it was not established for us to hallow it before all others, that is to count it more holy." [24]

The defined relation between the Sabbath and the Lord's Day, as well as the authority and process by which the latter was instituted, are questions that Calvin does not concern himself with here, even slightly. He gives no indication of his mind on these matters, but goes on immediately to discuss the obligations and proper use of the Lord's Day. His emphases are substantially those of the 1559 edition.

The primary purpose of the Lord's Day is that the church might have a day specifically set aside to assemble publicly, for common prayer, preaching, and the use of the sacraments. The Lord's Day is the day of public worship. "But it was established for the church to gather for prayers and praises of God, for hearing the Word, for the use of the sacraments." [24]

For believers to be better able to fulfill this obligation to worship, on the Lord's Day they properly cease from their daily occupations and any other labor or diversion that would tend to distract from the purpose of the day. "The better to devote all our efforts, singlemindedly to these tasks, we are to stop all mechanical and manual labor, and all pursuits which have to do with the conduct of this life." [24]

Whether or not Calvin considers this rest to be a specific obligation attaching to the fourth commandment is difficult to say. He immediately adds that all feast days fall under the same consideration (the propriety of resting from work on these days, as well as on the Lord's Day, to devote the time to public worship – a notion obviously not present in the teaching of the fourth commandment). "Of the same sort are other solemn days, wherein the mysteries of our salvation are called to mind." [24][41]

At any rate, what is paramount is that believers miss no opportunity for hearing the word, so that, by keeping the Sabbath in this way, on every day if possible, they may grow in sanctification and so continue to enjoy the eternal Sabbath. "But if we drink that Word wholeheartedly (as is fitting) and through it mortify the works of the old man, not only on festal days but every day continuously do we hallow the Sabbath; and, because we are here so commanded, we begin to celebrate Sabbath after Sabbath." [24][42]

In summarizing the demand of the fourth commandment for public worship, Calvin appeals here as in the definitive edition to the principle of decency and order set forth in I Corinthians 14. Sunday has not been set aside as the day of worship because it is inherently sacred, nor is God honored simply because we cease from toil on that day. Rather, it is fitting that the church assemble on any day of the week. Because, however, the ideal of daily gatherings is not practically possible, the first day of the week has been set aside as a day when believers may have the opportunity for coming together. This distinction is made solely out of a concern for order in the church and the desire to avoid chaos.

> To sum up: it is not by religion [non religione aliqua] that we distinguish one day from another, but for the sake of the common polity. For we have certain prescribed days not simply to celebrate, as if by our stopping labor God is honored and pleased, but because

it is needful for the church to meet together on a certain day. Moreover it is important for there to be a set and appointed day that all things may be done according to order and without disturbance (I Cor. 14). [24]

When the church keeps this purpose and use of the Lord's Day clearly in view, it will not become tainted by "the Jewish notion" [iudaica opinione] that the ceremonial part of the commandment has been abolished while the moral part still remains in force. [24] Clearly, as the discussion unfolds in almost identical language, Calvin has in mind here the view of the "false prophets" discussed later in the 1559 edition.[43] According to that view, the significance and obligations of the Old Testament Sabbath still remain in force. Only the day of the week on which this Sabbath is observed has been changed, from the seventh to the first. As he points out, both here and in the definitive edition, this amounts to changing the day out of contempt for the Jews while retaining a Jewish observance. Further, since it has not even the slightest sanction, it is a view that far surpasses the Jewish Sabbath in the superstitious abuses to which it is subject. "For those who cling to their constitutions surpass the Jews three times over in crass and carnal sabbatarian superstition." [24]

The Sabbath was instituted for Israel, he concludes, not only as a promissory sign of spiritual rest and a provision for a weekly day of worship, but also to give relief from labor and toil to servants and animals. "The Jews had another task to see to in sabbatarianism [sabbatismo spectandum], not one having to do with religion but with the preservation of equity among men. This means, actually, to remit the labor of servants and animals, lest inhuman taskmasters by persistent urging press them beyond due measure." [24]

This notion, though the third main emphasis of the 1559 edition, is hardly more than stated there. Here, however, there is the additional thought that respite from toil is more an advantage brought by the commandment than a reason for instituting it. "Moses was really pointing out the usefulness of something already taught rather than teaching something on his own (Exod. 23:11f.; Deut. 5:14f.)." [24][44] If such respite was provided for the Jews, his reasoning goes, then certainly it is to be enjoyed today by believers whose conduct is regulated by the law of love. "We are to have regard for equity today also, not out of any servile necessity, but according as love dictates." [24] That such physical rest is an advantage attendant on observing the Lord's Day rather than a reason for instituting it is a notion that we will encounter again.

Summary

The teaching of the 1536 edition of the *Institutes* may be summed up in the following propositions.

1. The weekly Sabbath was given to Israel as a type of spiritual rest from sin. At the coming of Christ, that rest became a reality and the Sabbath ceased to have typical significance. In that sense, the Sabbath has been abrogated. The present obligation of the fourth commandment is that believers strive daily to mortify the old man so that they might enjoy continual spiritual rest.

2. The weekly Sabbath was given to Israel to provide a day for public assembly and worship. In that respect the Lord's Day is related to the Sabbath, for the obligation to public worship equally binds Christian and Old Testament Jew. The Lord's Day, however, has not been set aside because of any inherent sanctity or because it has some typical significance. Rather, it has been designated as the day of public gathering for Christians solely out of a concern for maintaining order. Any day, or more than one day, of the week could have been chosen for that purpose.

3. The weekly Sabbath was given to Israel in order that servants and slaves might have periodic respite from toil and not be unjustly oppressed. That obligation, to provide laborers with special times for rest, is still in force today. Strictly speaking, physical rest is an ancillary benefit of keeping the fourth commandment rather than a reason for instituting it.

The Question of Development

Before turning to other material, we should address the question of development in Calvin's views on the Sabbath by comparing the teaching of the 1536 edition with that of the definitive edition. The answer to this question, which the reader perhaps can already anticipate, is not difficult: the slight development that can be detected is incidental; apart from the few differences already noted, the two editions agree entirely.

The question of development only comes into proper perspective when the first edition is compared with the second or 1539 edition. With the exception of a few additional fragments, the material of the 1559 edition is identical with that of 1539.[45] In effect, then, Calvin's Sabbath views, as far as they are expressed in the *Institutes*, were solidified by 1539.

That may be better appreciated if we note these additional fragments. The 1543 edition adds the two sentences at the beginning of chapter 8, section 34, "However, the ancients did not substitute the Lord's Day (as we call it) for the Sabbath without careful discrimination. The purpose and fulfillment of that true rest, represented by the ancient Sabbath, lies in the Lord's resurrection. Hence, by the very day that brought the shadows to an end, Christians are warned not to cling to the shadow rite."[46] This passage, as we noted earlier, introduces the notion that the Lord's Day was substituted for the Sabbath by the early church fathers.

In the 1545 edition the thought that private meditation as well as public worship is particularly appropriate on the Lord's Day, appears for the first time in the words, "... or at least to devote it particularly to meditation upon his works, and thus through this remembrance to be trained in piety," [395, section 28] and "... each one of us privately, whenever he has leisure, is to exercise himself diligently in pious meditation upon God's works." [400, section 34] Finally, unique to the 1559 edition is the summary statement at the very end of section 34, "But we ought especially to hold to this general doctrine: that, in order to prevent religion from either perishing or declining among us, we should diligently frequent the sacred meetings, and make use of those external aids which can promote the worship of God." [401]

These additions show the only really new idea that Calvin introduces after 1539 is private meditation, as well as public worship, as an appropriate exercise on the Lord's Day – hardly a thought that modifies his position in a way that may be considered basic.

His exposition in the definitive edition compared with the 1536 edition is not a contrast between two positions, one having grown out of the other after 23 years of continuous modification or even development. Rather, there are two positions, one appearing three years after the other and, apart from minor variations, remaining intact 20 years later and after several restatements in subsequent editions.[47]

Furthermore, this comparison shows that the two positions are fundamentally the same; they are, in fact, really one. Any differences that can be noted are plainly differences in emphasis rather than substance. Comparing the summary statements of the teaching of the 1559 and 1536 editions given earlier in this chapter, shows the basic identity of the two positions.

On the question of development, then, the conclusion is clear: So far as the teaching of the *Institutes* is concerned, Calvin's views on the fourth commandment first appear in 1536. Three years later these views are given a somewhat lengthier restatement, but any difference between the two editions is one of emphasis rather than substance. The material of the 1539 edition reappears almost verbatim in all of the subsequent editions, with only three minor additions introduced along the way. Calvin's view of the Sabbath or Lord's Day, it seems safe to say, was essentially determined by the time he was 27 years old, just over three years after his conversion, and he held virtually the same view some 23 years later, less than five years before his death. Furthermore, no evidence exists that in the intervening years he had doubts about or otherwise questioned that view.

Summary

Taking both the 1536 and 1559 editions together, the teaching of the *Institutes* may be broadly summarized as follows.

The fourth commandment, as an element of God's immutable Decalogue, is binding upon all men at all times. Its requirements are three fold.

1. The weekly Sabbath was given to Israel as a type of spiritual rest from sin. The rest of every seventh day was to stimulate their thinking upon the Lord, who would be their Sanctifier. At the coming of Christ, spiritual rest became a reality. The Sabbath then ceased to exist as a promissory sign and, consequently, no longer has typical significance for the Christian church. This does not mean, however, that this first requirement of the commandment no longer obligates the church. On the contrary, its demand is intensified. Christians must strive to cease from sinful works and thereby enter into and enjoy spiritual rest on every day of their lives.

2. The fourth commandment requires of the Christian church, as it required of Israel, that stated times be set aside for public worship. In the case of Israel the time was designated specifically by the Lord. For the church it is a matter of indifference which day of the week is chosen, although the first day, the day of the Resurrection, is most appropriate.

3. The fourth commandment requires of the Christian church, as it required of Israel, that rest be granted to all those who labor under the authority of others.

The Teaching of a *Short Creedal Statement* and a *Catechism*

1. *Catechism* (1538)[48]

The subtitle explains that this work, previously published in French for the Church in Geneva,[49] is now being made available in Latin to give it wider currency, so that it may be of benefit "to other churches everywhere."[50]

The title, *Catechism*, may give a misleading impression of the contents.[51] Though obviously written for purposes of instruction, it is not in the standard question-and-answer format. Rather, it consists of a number of brief statements on subjects at the heart of the Christian faith, and is more accurately described as a short creedal statement or a brief confession of faith.[52] Here, again, our concern is with an exposition of the fourth commandment, albeit a very brief one, as part of a treatment of the Decalogue. Its harmony with the teaching of the *Institutes* will be apparent.

Calvin begins by mentioning the reasons for the giving the commandment to Israel. These are the three by now familiar to us. First, the rest of the seventh day was given to typify spiritual rest. It encouraged the people to rest from their own sinful works and to look to the Lord, who would be their sanctifier. Secondly, the Sabbath provided a stated day on which the people might gather to hear the law and "carry out the ceremonies." [13][53] In the third place, God, by means of the Sabbath, granted a day of rest and respite from toil to everyone under the authority of another.[54]

There can be no doubt, he continues, that the first reason ceased to exist at the coming of Christ. For he is the truth in whose presence all figures disappear. The fact that the type has vanished, however, should not lead believers to conclude that this first reason no longer applies to their situation. Rather, its fulfillment brings to bear an obligation of the greatest importance. Christians are those who, according to Paul in Romans 6:8, have been buried with Christ, so that through his death, they might die to the corruption of their flesh. This dying with Christ and the resulting life (spiritual rest) it brings must be a daily endeavor. Such rest cannot be a concern confined to only one day of the week. "Superstitious observance of days ought therefore to be far from Christians." [13]

The two other reasons for giving the Sabbath to Israel ought not to be reckoned among the Old Testament types that have been abolished; they "fit all ages equally." [13] Although "the Sabbath was abrogated,"[55] still a day is properly set aside each week so that the church might assemble publicly for preaching, the use of the sacraments, and prayer, and so that a day of relief from work might be provided for servants and laborers.

Here, too, we find the same idea that appears in the 1559 edition. The ideal for the church is daily public assemblies for worship. Our weakness, however, prevents the realization of that ideal. "Yet such is our weakness that it cannot be arranged for meetings of this sort to take place daily."[56]

To the question how the principle of daily public worship may be deduced from the fourth commandment, or on what basis the commandment is seen as directed toward a situation arising from the failure to realize that principle, Calvin gives no answer. He simply goes on to assert that although, to avoid superstition, the day observed by the Jews was set aside, another day "was designated in its place,"[57] for maintaining "peace and order" in the church. [13] Nothing is said about the process or the authority by which the Lord's Day was established for this purpose.

Summary

Calvin's own conclusion may provide a summary here.[58]

The truth, delivered to the Jews under a figure, has been committed to the church without shadows.

1. Christians must practice a perpetual Sabbath through the whole of life, resting from their sinful works, so that God, through his Spirit, may work in them.

2. Christians must observe the lawful order of the church, constituted for preaching, for administering the sacraments, and for public prayers.

3. Christians must not inhumanly oppress those subject to their authority.

2. Genevan Catechism (1545)[59]

Probably because of its impractical form and the fact that shortly thereafter Calvin was driven from Geneva into exile, the *Catechism* of 1538 soon fell into disuse. Not surprisingly, then, shortly after his return to Geneva in 1541, many expressed the desire that Calvin provide them with a catechism suitable for instructing children and converts. He acknowledges such pressure in the prefatory letter to this second catechism, which appeared in November 1545. He states his preference for this catechism rather than the earlier one and his modest hope that it will prove useful for instructing those who are weak in the faith. [90]

Unlike its predecessor, this catechism has a question-and-answer format. On the whole it is better characterized as a dialogue (between "Minister" and "Child") than the crisp interrogation characteristic of most catechisms. The material in view here is a series of questions and answers dealing with the meaning of the ten commandments.

After replying to the Minister that the law is the "rule of life" God has given us, the Child, in response to the next question, states that the law "consists of two parts: the first of these contains four commandments, the other, six. So the whole law consists of ten commandments in all." [107] This interchange confirms, again, that any consideration of Calvin's teaching on the fourth commandment must remain aware that for him the Decalogue in all its parts is the law of God and is perpetually and universally binding.

Coming to the fourth commandment, the Child answers the Minister regarding the nature of the work forbidden: "This commandment has a distinct and peculiar ground. Since the observation of rest is part of the old ceremonies, it was therefore by the advent of Christ abrogated."

"Do you mean," the Minister resumes, "that this precept properly refers to the Jews, and so was merely temporary?"

"Yes," comes the reply, "so far as ceremonial is concerned."

"What then?" the Minister asks, "Is anything besides ceremonial subsumed under it?"

"It was given for three reasons," the Child replies. [111-12]

This interchange offers further indisputable proof that where Calvin speaks of the Sabbath having been abrogated or of the temporary character of the fourth commandment, such statements are immediately qualified. Qualification is most explicit here. Only the Sabbath narrowly considered in terms of its ceremonial character and the fourth commandment contemplated as prescribing this ceremony are said to be abolished. Furthermore, there is the additional proviso that more is involved in the fourth commandment than a ceremonial ordinance; "it was given for three reasons."

The "three reasons" the Child lists reflect the uniform emphasis we have encountered elsewhere. The fourth commandment has been given, "to symbolize spiritual rest; for the preservation of the ecclesiastical polity; for the relief of servants." [112] The Minister then seeks by his questions to encourage the Child to develop these themes.

Spiritual rest is "keeping holiday" from our own works that God may perform his works in us. It is realized by renouncing fleshly inclinations and accepting the guidance of the Holy Spirit. That is not something done sufficiently on one day of the week. On the contrary, once believers have begun spiritual rest, they must continue in it throughout the whole course of life.

If spiritual rest is to be an every day affair, "Why then is a certain day appointed to symbolize it." The reply: "There is no need for the reality to agree at all points with the symbol, if only it suit sufficiently for the purpose of symbolizing." [112]

Assuming that Calvin is speaking not of Israel's Sabbath but of the Sabbath to be kept by his readers, an apparently sound assumption in the light of the above quotations as well as the whole context, he is here using the idea of the Sabbath as a symbol in a way we have not previously encountered. Elsewhere we have seen that he uniformly speaks of the typical element as unique to the Old Testament's Sabbath and subsequently abolished at the advent of Christ. Here, however, he has in view a symbolic or figurative element in the Sabbath that Christians keep. Is he reversing himself on what he teaches in the *Institutes* and the *Catechism* of 1538?[60]

In fact, his remarks here shed light on a difficulty encountered in our discussion of the *Institutes*. There, on the one hand, he stresses the reality of spiritual rest as present since the first advent of Christ; at the same time, he speaks of that rest as not being fully realized until the Last Day. The solution to the apparent contradiction, proposed above,[61] is that these two benefits – the believers' present rest in Christ and eternal rest – were seen as so much the same, in principle, that he practically identified them.

That conclusion receives a good deal of support here as the dialogue continues. Having established that a day has been appointed to symbolize spiritual rest, the Minister continues by inquiring why it is that the seventh day was chosen. The answer gives two reasons. The first is one we have met before. Seven, in Scripture, is the number of perfection. Therefore it is suitable to indicate the perpetuity of the eternal Sabbath. Secondly, "it suggests that this spiritual rest only begins in this life, and does not reach perfection until we depart this world." [112]

Just how Calvin draws this latter reason from the number seven is a question, though interesting, we will not take up here. More importantly, on the assumption that the Sabbath Christians are to keep is in view here, this reason provides a clear statement that the Christian rest day is called a symbol because it indicates that spiritual rest is an actual possession yet will not be fully experienced until the Last Day. This indicates that our assumption that this notion is implicit in the *Institutes* is probably correct. To say that spiritual rest becomes a reality with Christ's first coming and then, a few sentences later, that it will not be realized until the Last Day, as Calvin does in the *Institutes*, is not to be guilty of inconsistency but to view the same rest in terms of different degrees of realization.[62]

When Calvin speaks of the symbolic significance of the Christian day of rest, he clearly means something different than when he calls Israel's Sabbath a type or ceremony. The latter prefigures spiritual rest. The former indicates that spiritual rest, already in possession, has yet to reach its final fulfillment.

This reference in the *Genevan Catechism* to the Christian rest day as a symbol may well reflect a degree of development in Calvin's thinking on the Sabbath. Curiously, this idea does not

appear elsewhere in his writings. Why it does not is difficult to
say. Perhaps he dropped it subsequently because he felt it was
misleading or at least subject to misunderstanding.

At any rate, the uniqueness of this additional idea can be
overemphasized. Whatever he does mean when he says that the
Lord's Day[63] is a symbol, clearly he is in no way toning down his
conviction that the typical character of Israel's Sabbath has been
abolished at the first advent of Christ. He is not saying that the
weekly rest day prefigures eternal rest, because, as he has stated
not only in the *Institutes* but also in this dialogue itself, such rest
is in principle already possessed by believers. Then, too, we
should presume that if he is here incorporating something
essentially new into his understanding of the fourth
commandment, that would find expression (which it does not) in
one of the editions of the *Institutes* subsequent to 1545.

My own judgment is that such language is an accommodation
for catechizing the unlearned. To call the Lord's Day a symbol
of spiritual rest simply underscores what Calvin emphasizes
elsewhere, namely that the Lord's Day serves to focus attention
on the fact that the spiritual rest foreshadowed to the Jews is now
an actual possession.[64]

As the dialogue continues, the Minister returns to the thought
he was emphasizing before branching off to discuss the Lord's
Day as a symbol. Spiritual rest, which means resting from sin so
that God may work in us, is not something to be done on only one
day of the week but continuously. To the question whether one
day each week is sufficient for meditating upon God's work and
resting from our own, the Child replies that every day ought to be
employed in such meditation, but that because of human
weakness, one day has been specially set aside. In answer to the
immediately following query as to the order to be kept on that
day: "The people [are] to meet for the hearing of Christian
doctrine, for the offering of public prayers, and for the
profession of their faith." [112] The emphasis falls, once again,
on the Lord's Day as a day of worship.[65]

The third main emphasis in the *Institutes* also finds

expression in this catechism. In reply to the question concerning what it means that the fourth commandment provides "for a relief of servants," the Child answers that a time of relaxation must be provided for all who are under the power of others. Interestingly, an additional thought appears, one we have not yet encountered in our study. If a day of rest is given to laborers, the answer continues, the order and productivity of society in general will be promoted. "For when one day is assigned for rest, everyone accustoms himself to work the rest of the time." [113]

Summary

The teaching of the *Geneva Catechism* agrees completely with the teaching of the *Institutes* and the *Catechism* of 1538. Certain minor differences of emphasis exist, but those in no way affect the more fundamental and pervasive harmony. The final lines of the dialogue provide, in Calvin's own words, the best summary of its teaching. [113]

> Minister: Let us see how far this command refers to us.
>
> Child: As to ceremony, since its reality existed in Christ, I hold it to be abrogated (Col. 2:20).
>
> M: How?
>
> C: Just because our old nature is by virtue of his death crucified, and we are raised up to newness of life.
>
> M: How much of the commandment then remains for us?
>
> C: Not to neglect the sacred ordinances which contribute to the spiritual polity of the church; especially to attend the sacred assemblies for the hearing of the Word of God, the celebration of the mysteries, and the regular prayers as they will be ordained.
>
> M: But does the symbol [figura] lead us no further?
>
> C: Certainly: for it calls us to the reality behind it, namely, that being grafted into the body of Christ and made members of his, we cease from our own works and so resign ourselves to the government of God.[66]

References

1. J. T. McNeill, *The History and Character of Calvinism* (New York: Oxford University Press, 1954), p. 93.

2. See above, p. 12.

3. Hessey, *Sunday*, p. 172.

4. In the Lutheran division of the Decalogue, followed by Zahn here, the Sabbath commandment is the third.

5. T. Zahn, "Geschichte des Sonntags," *Skizzen aus dem Leben der Alten Kirche* (Erlangen and Leipzig, 1894), p. 237.

6. Gilfillan, *The Sabbath*, p. 426.

7. P. Fairbairn, *The Typology of Scripture*, 2 (Grand Rapids: Zondervan, n.d.): 458.

8. A. Kuyper, *Tractaat van den Sabbath* (Amsterdam: Wormser, 1890), pp. 81 ff. These pages also contain a citation and discussion of Voetius' position. Cf. W. Geesink, *Gereformeerde Ethiek*, 1 (Kampen: Kok, 1931): 359-60.

9. L. Praamsma, "Calvijn over de Sabbath," *Church and Nation*, 6 (Nov. 28, 1961): 91-92.

10. See the brief overview of this observation, above, pp. 14-20.

11. J. Calvin, *Institutes of the Christian Religion*, 1 (ed. J. McNeill, trans. F. Battles; *The Library of Christian Classics*, vol. 20, London: SCM Press, 1961): 398-99. Hereafter cited as *Institutes*. Unless otherwise noted, all quotations are from this translation. Subsequent citations will also be given in the standard form, i.e., by book, chapter, section.

12. "Calvijn over de Sabbath," p. 92, col. 3 ("... hij een zeer nauwgezet en eerlijk exegeet was").

13. A brief section on two sermons, which I was unable to deal with in my 1962 thesis, will follow treatment of the commentary material.

14. See B.B. Warfield, "On the Literary History of Calvin's Institutes," *Calvin and Calvinism* (New York: Oxford University Press, 1931), pp. 373-428, and the comments of McNeill in the "Introduction" to *Institutes*, 1: xxix-xxxviii. The following remarks are based on information gleaned largely from these two sources. See, more recently, the "Chronological Index of Calvin's Writings," in W. de Greef, *The Writings of John Calvin. An Introductory Guide* (trans. L. Bierma; Grand Rapids: Baker, 1993 [1989]), pp. 237-41.

15. *Institutes*, 1: 394-401 (2:8:28-34); page numbers for

subsequent quotations will be in the main text [in brackets].

16. J. Calvinus, *Institutio Christianae Religionis* (Geneva, 1559), *Opera Selecta* [=OS] (ed. P. Barth and G. Niesel; München: Chr. Kaiser, 1957), 3: 370 (2:8:28). I will cite the Latin text only where the English translation is imprecise or the Latin is worth noting. All Latin citations from the 1559 edition are from this source. Since these will always be made in connection with use of the English translation, which is cited by book, chapter and section, there generally will be no need for separate referencing of the Latin.

17. Whether quoting directly or citing indirectly, I will not usually include all the Scriptural references Calvin does.

18. Except perhaps in his sermons on Deuteronomy 5:12-15, see below, chapter 3.

19. See above, p. 25; more recently, P. Jewett, *The Lord's Day* (Grand Rapids: Eerdmans, 1971), pp. 102-06 (for Calvin, Sabbath observ-ance is "expedient, rather than mandatory," p. 106); J. Primus, *Holy Time. Moderate Puritanism and the Sabbath* (Macon, GA: Mercer, 1989), pp. 126, 132 ["Calvin and the Puritan Sabbath: A Comparative Study," in ed. D. Holwerda, *Exploring the Heritage of John Calvin* (Grand Rapids: Baker, 1976), pp. 64, 72] (God's rest after creating is no more than "an alluring example for both Jews and Christians to follow," p. 132 [=p. 72]); Bauckham, with a somewhat different overall appraisal, observes, parenthetically, "... only in his commentary on Genesis does he treat it [the Christian observance of a weekly day of rest for worship] as a creation ordinance" ("Sabbath and Sunday in the Protestant Tradition," p. 317). Although it is certainly true, as we will see, that Calvin does not find a weekly, one-day-in-seven Sabbath any longer required for Christians by the fourth commandment, such assessments, as the preceding, fail to appreciate that here, in the *Institutes*, he does appeal to God's creation rest within a context of explaining how Sabbath observance, *as mandated by the fourth commandment*, obligates the church today. That this appeal results in a certain tension in his overall view of the Sabbath is a matter we will take up in detail below.

20. See the brief sketch of these practices given above in the latter part of chapter 1, pp. 19-20.

21. It is perhaps not superfluous to say that this mention of abrogation should not be pressed beyond what Calvin intended.

Obviously he is referring to the Sabbath as a type; in that sense specifically it is abolished.

22. Primus ("Calvin and the Puritan Sabbath," p. 62, n. 100), believes that this sentence, which he (slightly mis-)quotes from my 1962 thesis (and without noting the qualification provided by the immediately following sentence), "puts it too strongly." But surely a main point of section 32 is that public worship is one of "[t]he two latter reasons for the Sabbath" (mentioned also as one of the three major reasons previously, in section 28) that "are equally applicable in every age." Surely, too, the editor of the Battles' translation is correct in supplying the heading to section 32 (taken over from the German translation of Otto Weber), "How far does the *Fourth Commandment* go beyond external regulation?" (emphasis added). Note as well the final sentence of Calvin's entire exposition of the fourth commandment [401].

23. It is worth noting that in the Latin text the word for "rule" or "commandment" is "ratio" rather than "praeceptum," "mandatum" or "ordinatio," terms that are much stronger and that Calvin uniformly uses in referring to divine precepts or injunctions (including the fourth commandment).

24. In a footnote (40) at the bottom of this page, the editor, J. T. McNeill, discusses an incident that may have prompted Calvin's reply to the "restless spirits." He cites a letter from a minister in Thonon to the ministers in Geneva, who refers to the imprisonment of a Genevan citizen, Colinaeus, for unorthodox opinions on baptism and the Sabbath.

25. See above, p 25.

26. He quotes from or paraphrases Colossians 2:17; Galatians 4:10-11; Romans 14:5.

27. The Latin original in both contexts is "veteres."

28. The Latin "taxatio" can take the meanings, "valuing," "esteeming." Either of these would give a slightly stronger force than "appointing." The Allen translation has "appointment," Beveridge, "taxation."

29. In the view of A. Lincoln, "Aquinas' formulation of the issues were [sic] in turn determinative for the Reformers who did not break with his basic premises, though Luther and Calvin resisted their logic, and for both Puritan Sabbatarianism and nineteenth century English

Sabbatarianism, which continued the tradition of Sabbath-transference theology" (*From Sabbath to Lord's Day*, p. 390); cf. the similar assessment of Bauckham (pp. 312-17): "Moreover we should not exaggerate the extent to which the Reformers broke with the *premises* of scholastic Sabbatarianism" (312, emphasis original); "The Reformers' break with medieval Sabbatarianism was not complete; ...." (317). Such statements, read in their contexts, are misleading at best, because they do not take into account the radical discontinuity in soteriological and overall theological framework, for viewing the Decalogue and the Sabbath, between medieval Catholicism and the Reformers (and, in continuity with them, subsequent Protestant orthodoxy).

30. The secondary literature here is legion. I make no effort to cite or interact with it.

31. The words "The ten commandments," in parentheses, are joined to the title in the Battles translation (*Institutes*, 1: 367). They do not, however, appear in the original.

32. The immediate context makes clear that the law of the two tables is still in view.

33. *Institutes*, 2: 1503 (4:20:15).

34. Cf. A. Pieters, "Three Views of the Fourth Commandment," *The Calvin Forum*, 6 (Jan. 1941): 119-121; "Calvin's View of the Fourth Commandment," *The Calvin Forum*, 7 (Aug.-Sept., 1941): 22-25 for an attempt to show that Calvin, particularly in the *Institutes*, teaches the abrogation of the fourth commandment.

35. J. Calvin, *Institutes of the Christian Religion* (trans. F. Battles; Grand Rapids: Meeter Center/Eerdmans, 1989), p. 15; pp. 23-25 for treatment of the fourth commandment (further quotations will be cited with the page reference in brackets in the text). This, apparently, is the first and only English translation of this edition (first printing, with different pagination, Atlanta: John Knox, 1975). For the Latin original, J. Calvinus, *Christianae Religionis Institutio* (Basilea: 1536), OS, 1 (ed. P. Barth; München: Chr. Kaiser; 1926); pp. 46-49 deal with the fourth commandment (the text of the English translation includes the pagination for the Latin, between forward slashes) .

36. More specifically, Galatians 4:8-11 and Colossians 2:16-17, as Battles proposes, are likely intended.

37. At the risk of appearing unduly repetitious, this passage clearly

illustrates again the need to take Calvin's more controversial statements on the Sabbath in their context. Consequently, the widespread perception, especially among scholars, to the effect that Calvin teaches that the fourth commandment does not apply to Christians, is puzzling. As the above quotations once again make clear, nothing could be farther from his mind.

38. *Institutes*, 1:397 (2:28:31).

39. "last" [tunc tandem].

40. "assidue" ("continuously," "untiringly," "incessantly").

41. Calvin's view on feast days is difficult to know exactly. When he first arrived in Geneva, he was apparently in agreement with the action of Viret and Farel, who had already had them banned. Moreover, he was later exiled for opposing the demand of the Bernese government to reintroduce the observation of Christmas, Easter, Ascension Day, and Pentecost. Upon his eventual return to Geneva, with these feast days again being observed, he did not oppose them, but only warned against equating them with Sunday. Several years later, however, when a majority of the ministers opposed them, he used his influence to have them banned again. Probably, we should conclude, though he did not favor them, he tolerated feast days as long as they were not used superstitiously. Cf. Geesink, *Gerefomeerde Ethiek* (Kampen: Kok, 1931), 1: 374; *Van's Heeren Ordination* (Kampen: Kok, n.d.), 1: 568; McNeill, *History and Character of Calvinism*, pp. 142, 165.

42. The phrase "sabbatum ex sabbato," an obvious reflection upon Isaiah 66:23, Calvin takes as a prophecy of the eternal Sabbath. The sentence quoted is yet another indication how, in his view, the believer's present rest from sin is to be identified in principle with eternal rest.

43. See above, pp. 43-44.

44. This translation seems to shift the provision of equitable rest for laborers away from the fourth commandment in a way Calvin did not intend. To translate less freely, "Nevertheless this, as I judge, is pointed out by Moses (Exod. 23; Deut. 5) as an advantage of the institution rather than the reason for instituting it." ("Quamquam haec, ut arbitror, magis instituti utilitas a Mose indicabatur [Exod. 23, Deut. 5], quam instituendi causa.")

45. Just one of the helpful features of the Battles' translation is that, among existing English translations, it alone provides the reader with

the editorial apparatus necessary for properly appreciating the above observations. The *Opera Selecta* edition provides the same apparatus. That the 1559 edition deletes nothing from the 1539 edition can only be verified in Latin; for the 1539 edition, see *Ioannis Calvini Opera Quae Supersunt Omnia* [=CO], 1 (ed. G. Baum, E. Cunitz, E. Reuss; Brunsvigae: Schwetschke et Filium, 1866): 401-406.

46. *Institutes*, I:399-400.

47. It is worth noting that not only the exposition of the fourth commandment but the entire eighth chapter of Book 2 had taken more or less final form by the 1539 edition. That may be easily verified by scanning the contents of the chapter in the Battles' translation.

48. Trans. F. Battles in I. Hesselink, *Calvin's First Catechism. A Commentary* (Louisville, KY: Westminster John Knox, 1997), pp. 1-38, on the Sabbath, 12-13; *Catechismus* (Basilea: 1538), CO, 5: 313-62, on the Sabbath, 328-29.

49. J. Calvin, *Instruction in Faith (1537)*; trans. and ed. P. Fuhrmann (Louisville, KY: Westminster/John Knox, 1992); *Instruction et Confession de Foy*, OS, 1: 378-417.

50. *Calvin's First Catechism*, p. 1.

51. The expanded title is *Catechism or Institution [Institutio] of the Christian Religion*.

52. As the title of the French edition shows (see n. 49).

53. Presumably aspects of the Levitical ritual are in view.

54. The French edition adds, missing from the Latin, that this third reason is "rather an inferred than a principal reason" (Fuhrmann, *Instruction*, p. 31); "... plustost une dependence que rayson principale" (OS, 1: 385). This thought, as we will see later, is developed at some length in the second of Calvin's two sermons on the fourth commandment in Deuteronomy 5.

55. This assertion is qualified by the immediate context, which makes abundantly clear that in view specifically is abrogation of the typical character of the Sabbath. Here (as elsewhere) there is no basis for the notion that Calvin teaches that the fourth commandment is no longer in force.

56. Cf. *Institutes*, 1:398 (2:8:32) and the discussion above, pp. 37-38.

57. "... in eum usum destinatus est," CO, 5: 329.

58. The paraphrase that follows here varies at several places (cf. CO, 5: 329) from Battles' translation.

59. J. Calvin, *Catechism of the Church of Geneva* (trans. J. K. S. Reid, *Calvin: Theological Treatises*; *The Library of Christian Classics*, 22 [London: SCM, 1954]), pp. 83-139; for the Latin original, ed. P. Barth and D. Schevner, *Opera Selecta*, 2 (München: Chr. Kaiser, 1952): 59-157. An earlier version in French appeared in 1542.

60. The Latin word "figura," which appears in this context several times and is translated "symbol," is the same word used elsewhere to indicate that the typical or figurative character of the (Old Testament) Sabbath has been abolished; cf., e.g., CO, 3: 373 [2:8:31]; OS, 1: 47.

61. See above, pp. 35-36, 51-52.

62. The real difficulty in this section of the *Genevan Catechism* is that Calvin talks as if the Christian rest day is the seventh day of the week. If that were true, it would completely contradict the teaching of the *Institutes*, or for that matter, any of his other writings available to us. As we already seen, he preferred Sunday, but would not oppose the selection of any other day (*Institutes*, 1: 400). Probably, we should conclude that he composed this dialogue strictly in terms of the language of the fourth commandment and expects that his readers will apply what he says to the day Christians now observe.

63. It is true that "Lord's Day" is not used in the Genevan Catechism, but when his remarks are about the day of rest that Christians keep, he is clearly speaking of the Lord's Day.

64. See *Institutes*, 1: 399-400 (2:8:34).

65. Note that here again Calvin deduces the ideal of daily public worship from the believer's obligation to practice a constant meditation upon God's work (i.e., spiritual rest), and understands the fourth commandment as accommodation to human weakness that makes the realization of this ideal impossible; cf. *Institutes*, 1: 398 (2:8:32) and above, pp. 37-38.

66. This answer substantiates our conclusion above that Calvin, when speaking of the Lord's Day as a symbol, has it in mind as a reminder of spiritual rest already in possession, rather than a prefiguration of that rest.

Chapter 3

Exegetical Writings and Sermons

Scripture contains a number of references to the Sabbath and the fourth commandment. Calvin discusses many of these in his numerous commentaries. Much of that exegetical comment will be examined in this chapter to see how it comports with his teaching elsewhere, especially in the *Institutes*, and with conclusions reached in the preceding chapter.

The Teaching of the Commentaries[1]

•*Genesis 2:3*
Calvin's comments on this verse have already been referred to indirectly. Toward the beginning of the previous chapter, we noted that Voetius, Abraham Kuyper and, more recently, Louis Praamsma, all find a contradiction between what he says in commenting on this verse and what he teaches in the *Institutes*.[2] They argue that in the *Institutes*, the day or days of the week the church chooses for public worship is a matter of indifference, while in the *Commentaries on Genesis*, one day in seven is to be the day of worship.

With certain qualifications, our study has shown the former part of this argument to be correct. Calvin does indeed say that he will "not condemn churches that have other solemn days for their meetings."[3] That statement, however, appears just after he has stated his own preference for the Lord's Day as the weekly day of worship. Still, the question remains whether the latter contention above is correct. Does the *Commentaries on Genesis* teach that the Christian church is obligated to keep one day in seven as the day of worship? An affirmative answer would show that Calvin does contradict himself, and at a fairly basic level.

A plausible case can be made that he does teach that the New Testament church is bound to keep one day out of seven as its day of rest and worship. In discussing what it means that God has "blessed the seventh day and made it holy" (v. 3), he notes, among other considerations, that "every seventh day has been especially selected for the purpose of supplying what was wanting in daily meditation." A little later he adds that God "dedicated every seventh day to rest, that his own example might be a perpetual rule"; and again, "God did not command men simply to keep holiday every seventh day, as if he delighted in their indolence, ..."[4]

Each of these three excerpts contains the phrase, "every seventh day."[5] So it might seem that one day of the week has been singled out to be kept by Christians as the weekly rest, without specifying what day that is. The contention of Voetius, Kuyper, and Praamsma (Calvin here teaches the "one-day-in-seven" principle) would appear to be well founded.

"Every seventh day," however, may be understood in another way. It could also mean that the seventh or last day, specifically, is to be kept as the weekly day of rest and worship.

"Every seventh day," then, may mean either that one day out of seven is to be kept as a Sabbath, without specifying the particular day of the week, or that specifically the last day is to be kept as the weekly Sabbath. How are we to tell which alternative is truly Calvin's?

At a first glance, his comments may not seem to provide an answer. The ambiguity, apparently, will have to be resolved, if possible, in the light of other considerations. A careful look at the context, however, reveals a different, more promising picture.

The material pertinent to the question just posed is a single long paragraph commenting on the beginning of verse 3, "And God blessed the seventh day." Few, if any, will disagree that this clause refers specifically to the seventh day and not, more generally, to one day in seven. That favors the presumption that when Calvin speaks of "every seventh day," he means specifically the seventh day, unless there were clear indications to the contrary. Such, apparently, there are not.

Further, as his exposition unfolds, he discusses what it means that God "sanctified" the seventh day. That divine activity he clearly considers relevant to all people, not simply to the Old Testament Jews.[6] "God therefore sanctifies the seventh day [diem septimum], when he renders it illustrious, that by a special law it may be distinguished from the rest." [105] Here, clearly, he is talking about the seventh day and not one day in seven. And a few lines later, he remarks, "Wherefore, that benediction is nothing else than a solemn consecration, by which God claims for himself the meditations and employments of men on the seventh day [die septimo]." [105] Again, specifically the seventh day is plainly in view.

A few lines further, in the same context and with the same emphasis on the meaning for humanity that God has sanctified the seventh day, the three references to the phrase, "every seventh day," cited above, begin to appear. Therefore this phrase, since he uses it not only in close proximity to but also with the same force as "the seventh day" (which, as we have seen, clearly refers specifically to the seventh day), not only includes the bare notion of one day in seven but also refers specifically to the seventh day.

If this conclusion is valid, then the question of a contradiction in Calvin stands in a rather different light. A contradiction, if such exists, between the *Institutes* and the Genesis commentary is no longer between the notions that any day is appropriate for Christian worship and that one day out of seven has been set aside for worship. Rather, the contradiction now appears to be that according to the *Institutes,* which day of the week Christians choose for worship is an indifferent matter, while the *Genesis* commentary teaches that God has set aside the seventh day specifically for worship. To put the issue another way, which underscores the apparent conflict more sharply: Calvin would be saying in one place that Christians are free to choose their day of worship; in another, that God has mandated the seventh day for worship.

This is the only plausible case that can be made for conflict between Calvin's teaching in the *Institutes* (and elsewhere) and the Genesis commentary. Yet it is doubtful whether anyone would seriously entertain that such a conflict exists. For there is not the slightest evidence, from either his other writings or the practices of the church at Geneva, to support, even remotely, the idea that he held that the seventh day is to be kept as the weekly Christian day of worship.

To entertain the notion either that Calvin taught that the seventh day, specifically, is the day of worship or that he argued that one day in seven is to be set aside for worship, is to misapprehend the basic thrust of his teaching on the fourth commandment, teaching, as we will presently see, that is in fact reflected in the very same paragraph where contradiction to it is supposed to be introduced. For him, to insist that Christians are bound by either of the above alternatives (one day in seven or the seventh day specifically) would be nothing less than to reintroduce a Jewish ceremony.

God's enduring purpose in sanctifying the seventh day was to provide an example for all people. "For God cannot either more gently allure, or more effectually incite us to obedience, than by inviting and exhorting us to the imitation of himself." Such imitation means "to celebrate the justice, wisdom, and power of God, and to consider his benefits .... " [106]

This brings us very close to his fundamental notion of spiritual rest. But, he has told us repeatedly elsewhere, believers are to cultivate such rest daily. Here, too, he says, "Spiritual rest is the mortification of the flesh; so that the sons of God should no longer live unto themselves, or indulge their own inclinations." [107] That hardly has in view, on any construction, what is confined to only one day of the week. Much less, then, can he mean that public worship, the appropriate expression of spiritual resting, is to be similarly confined to one day of the week.[7]

Calvin's intention in this passage may be gotten at in another way. "[I]n the Law," he says, "a new precept concerning the Sabbath was given, which should be peculiar to the Jews, and but for a season; because it was a legal ceremony shadowing forth a spiritual rest, the truth of which has been manifest in Christ." [106]

His view of the Decalogue will not allow the conclusion that he is saying here that the heart of the fourth commandment was given for the first time at Sinai. Rather, his thought, most likely, is that for the Jews a typical element was attached to the keeping of the commandment, and that this typical element, involving the obligation to rest on the seventh day of each week from labor, lost its force at the coming of Christ. To put it even more succinctly, apparently for Calvin the language of the fourth commandment, which speaks of six days of labor to be followed by the seventh day of rest from all labor, is historically conditioned and is not integral for stating the essence of the precept.

Admittedly, this interpretation is not without its problems. Two statements, in particular, pose difficulties.

> Therefore when we hear that the Sabbath was abrogated by the coming of Christ, we must distinguish between what belongs to the perpetual government of human life, and what properly belongs to the ancient figures, the use of which was abolished when the truth was fulfilled....
>
> So far as the Sabbath was a figure of rest, I say, it was but for a season; but inasmuch as it was commanded to men from the beginning that they might employ themselves in the worship of God, it is right that it should continue to the end of the world. [106-07]

What element in the Sabbath institution "belongs to the perpetual government of human life"? What is the Sabbath that "was commanded to men from the beginning" and which "should continue to the end of the world"?

Such language, it may seem, can only mean that Calvin has in mind some perpetual and universally binding principle establishing the ratio of days of work to day of rest. Further, the "one-day-in-seven" principle would appear to be the most likely candidate, and so he does, after all, contradict what he says in the *Institutes*.

Before accepting that conclusion, however, another question needs to be considered. What evidence is there, either in this commentary or elsewhere in Calvin supporting the conclusion that these quotations allude to the "one-day-in-seven" principle. Someone convinced that Genesis 2:3 teaches that the essence of the fourth commandment is the perpetual obligation to set aside one day each week for rest and worship, may well be inclined to find an allusion to that principle in Calvin's words. But is that really what he had in mind?

Our own reflections on this verse have already shown an insurmountable difficulty confronting the supposition that he teaches the "one-day-in-seven" principle. The ambiguous phrase, "every seventh day" (which may seem plausibly to express this principle), when seen in the light of other usage in the context, can only mean specifically the seventh day of each week.[8] That consideration, then, should govern the question immediately under discussion. If Calvin is here really laying down the ratio of days of work to day of rest, then this "perpetual government of human life" which "should continue to the end of the world," can only be the abiding obligation to keep the seventh day of each week for rest and worship.

But this conclusion, as already noted, is manifestly implausible, if not impossible. Nowhere, either elsewhere in his writings or the practice of the church at Geneva, is there the slightest ground for the idea that he taught that Christians are obligated to keep the seventh day of the week for rest and worship.

The difficulties in Calvin's language can be more easily resolved, if the equivocation possible on the word "Sabbath" is taken into account. Most of his subsequent readers, certainly today, immediately associate the word with the day each week set aside for worship and rest from labor. With Calvin, however, the association of "Sabbath" is not so much with a day as with a principle or guiding rule.

Consequently, when he says that the Sabbath "should continue to the end of the world" and belongs "to the perpetual government of human life," he is not thinking specifically of a weekly day of rest and worship but rather of a principle or ideal. If we ask what that ideal is, the core of the fourth commandment is the obvious answer. And that core the *Institutes* state quite clearly: practicing a perpetual rest from sin, meditating privately upon God's works whenever possible, observing the times of public worship "set by the church," and not overburdening laborers.[9]

An analogous consideration, drawn from another of the 10 commandments, may help to clarify Calvin's meaning. Although all that the fifth commandment requires explicitly is that children respect their parents, many will agree, for instance, with answer 64 of the *Westminster Shorter Catechism,* that "The fifth commandment requireth the preserving the honor, and performing the duties, belonging to everyone in their several places and relations, as superiors, inferiors, or equals." Similarly, this commandment does not promise Christians longevity in the land of Canaan. Rather, its promise is to be understood more generally, as does Paul in Ephesians 6:2-3 and, following him, answer 66 of the *Shorter Catechism*, as "a promise of long life and prosperity (as far as it shall serve for God's glory, and their own good) to all such as keep this commandment."

In the same vein is Calvin's approach to the language of the fourth commandment. The literal demand that the first six days of the week be devoted to labor and the seventh to rest was an obligation binding upon God's people in Old Testament times only. But the core of the commandment (noted above), he says, applies to all and "should continue to the end of the world." This also explains why he can speak of the sanctifying the seventh day in the most universal terms, as he does in this commentary, when his own practice and teaching elsewhere make clear that he did not consider Christians bound to rest and worship on that day. As in the *Genevan Catechism,* so here in the Genesis commentary, he conducts his exposition strictly in terms of the language of the text and expects his readers to apply his remarks to the particular day of the week which, for whatever reasons, they have chosen to set apart for worship and rest. To repeat and to summarize: the core of the fourth commandment and the Sabbath idea is what Calvin has in mind in this passage; for him that core does not involve the obligation to keep either one day in seven or the seventh day specifically as a day of rest and worship.

This interpretation may be difficult for some to accept. I want to underscore that I have arrived at it proceeding on the supposition, sound it seems to me, that internal conflict in Calvin is highly improbable. I have approached the Genesis commentary in the light of the *Institutes*, anticipating that the former could be best explained in the light of the latter.

This approach does not distort the teaching of the commentary. Calvin's exposition of Genesis 2:3 is very brief and fragmentary and, therefore, when considered solely in terms of itself, allows a variety of interpretations, all of which are not necessarily consistent with each other. For this reason, it is hardly improper to consider the commentary material in the light of the much more comprehensive and exhaustive statement, maintained consistently in successive editions, of the *Institutes*. Taking this approach and expecting to find harmony does not appear to abuse the material of the commentary or make Calvin say something he did not mean.

With that said, however, a qualification or, perhaps better, addition is needed to round out the present discussion. As pointed out earlier, in the *Institutes* Calvin is very clear in maintaining that, although he cannot bind anyone on the basis of the fourth commandment to keep Sunday as their day of rest and worship, he favors the observance of the Lord's Day.[10] That preference, coupled with his conviction concerning the seventh day idea in Scripture, which again he will not force on those who consider it "too subtle,"[11] shows that he had the greatest sympathy with, even preference for, what later came to be known as the "one-day-in-seven" principle. So, without undermining our conclusions above or introducing an element of contradiction between his teaching in the *Institutes* and in the Genesis commentary, we may fairly find in the mention the latter makes of the Sabbath as a "perpetual government of human life" which "should continue to the end of the world," an allusion to his preference for the rule, in practice, that one day each week should be set aside for rest and worship.

Before leaving the material of the Genesis commentary, two further points, perhaps already noted by the reader, should be highlighted. First, from the material quoted, Calvin clearly maintains, as he does elsewhere, that the Sabbath given to Israel was a figure of spiritual rest. It was "a symbol of sanctification [sanctificationis symbolum] to his ancient people." [106] In his customary way, he speaks of the abrogation of the Sabbath, by which he plainly means the abrogation, at Christ's coming, of this typical element (105-06, already quoted above).

This leads to a second observation. This commentary provides the clearest evidence that for Calvin the fourth commandment given at Sinai reflects a creation ordinance and, therefore, is perpetually binding on all. As I have already demonstrated, in discussing the material in the *Institutes*,[12] his appraisal of the Decalogue permitted him no other view. But here the grounding of this commandment in creation is stated explicitly. Not only is our obligation to keep Sabbath based upon God's sanctification of the seventh day; he says expressly, "but inasmuch as it [the Sabbath] was commanded to men from the beginning . . . , it is right that it should continue to the end of the world." [106]

•*Exodus 20:8-11/Deuteronomy 5:12-15*
Comments on these two versions of the Decalogue and on other verses below from the Pentateuch are from the *Commentaries on the Four Last Books of Moses.*

"The object of this commandment is that believers should exercise themselves in the worship of God."[13] Calvin begins his exposition by emphasizing, as elsewhere, that a fundamental concern of the fourth commandment is to facilitate worship. He then discusses the place of the Sabbath in the Old Testament system of feasts and ceremonies. Along with these festivals, it provided times of public assembly for sacrifices, prayers, and praise.

The Sabbath, however, possessed a uniqueness that set it apart within Israel's ceremonial system and explains why the Sabbath is commanded in the Decalogue. That uniqueness is the "spiritual substance," of which the Sabbath was the type. The Jewish Sabbath was a figure of spiritual rest. The rest of every seventh day was a promise that God would give his people rest from sin. As he puts it in the Genesis commentary, the Sabbath was a "symbol of sanctification." It was a sign that distinguished Israel from all other nations; God would be their sanctifier.

In a manner already familiar to us, he next argues at some length that spiritual rest has become a full reality with the advent of Christ so that the typical element in the Jewish Sabbath has been abolished. In this connection, however, he introduces an important additional thought not yet encountered in the works we have so far examined.

Only by taking into account the typical character of the Old Testament Sabbath and the magnitude of its subsequent antitypical fulfillment, Calvin maintains, can one understand the rigor with which Sabbath violations were punished under the old dispensation. "Moreover, if there had not been some peculiar excellency in the Sabbath, it might have appeared to be an act of atrocious injustice to condemn a man to be put to death for cutting wood upon it." [435] That "peculiar excellency" resides in the significance of the Sabbath as a figure of sanctification. To fail to observe the type was to forfeit the reality and so subjected the guilty one to the most extreme condemnation and display of divine wrath.

In this connection he makes a related point, one we have already met with elsewhere but I have not emphasized sufficiently. The command to rest on every seventh day demanded more of the Israelites than mere physical inactivity. It was not a blind, purposeless cessation from labor, but involved the obligation to meditate upon the spiritual significance and promise typified by that rest.

> Surely God has no delight in idleness and sloth, and therefore there was no importance in the simple cessation of the labors of their hands and feet; nay, it would have been a childish superstition to rest with no other view than to occupy their repose in the service of God. [434][14]

Here Calvin again takes up the question of the seventh day, "why God rather assigned every seventh day to the Sabbath rather than the sixth or tenth." [436] And here again, it is worth reminding ourselves, this discussion is carried on in terms of the language of the fourth commandment. In other words, strictly speaking, he is talking about the Jewish Sabbath, unless he specifically indicates otherwise.

His comments follow the general lines already laid down in the *Institutes*.[15] Seven is the Scriptural number of perfection. Therefore in relation to the Sabbath it may have either one of two slightly different meanings. It may mean that believers are to strive after perfect holiness and not be content with half-way measures in their lives. Or it may signify that the goal of sanctity involves an unending quest, that we must strive for it all the days of our lives.

Regardless of how his readers may assess these two suggestions, there can be no doubting that God rested on the seventh day, "that He might give a manifestation of the perfect excellency of His works, and thus, proposing Himself as the model of our imitation, He signifies that He calls His own people to the true goal of felicity." [436] Broadly speaking, then, the fourth commandment is a call to all believers to be followers and imitators of God; more particularly, the Sabbath given to Israel was a promise of sanctification. "He promises indeed that as He blessed the seventh day and set it apart, so He will bless believers to sanctify them." [437]

The main point, he continues, is the command, not the promise. "There is indeed no moment which should be allowed to pass in which we are not attentive to the consideration of the wisdom, power, goodness, and justice of God in His admirable creation and government of the world." [437] But because of the weakness and sinful inclinations of human nature man is incapable of such perpetual meditation. Therefore, God set aside the seventh day of each week as a day of rest from all earthly labors and concerns, so that the people of Israel might freely devote themselves to "that holy occupation." This "holy occupation" involved both private rest and public assembly. "On this ground He did not merely wish that people should rest at home, but that they should meet in the sanctuary, there to engage themselves in prayer and sacrifices, and to make progress in religious knowledge through the interpretation of the Law." [437]

"In this respect," he immediately adds, "we have an equal necessity for the Sabbath with the ancient people, so that on one day we may be free, and thus the better prepared to learn and to testify our faith." [437] Here is another statement that may appear to contradict what he says in the *Institutes*. The difficulty, however, is no greater than that encountered in his comments on Genesis 2:3, and the approach we adopted there ought to be followed here.

Plainly Calvin is not asserting that Christians are bound to observe the day the Jews kept. Nor is there the slightest evidence, either in this statement or its context, that he has in mind the "one-in-seven" principle as obligatory. Rather, he is simply stating that since Christians are subject to the same weaknesses as the Jews, a day each week needs to be set aside for rest from work so that all may gather at the same time for public worship as well as have ample opportunity for unimpeded private meditation. Which day of the week this is or the frequency with which it is to be observed are matters not touched on. This statement conforms fully with the teaching of the *Institutes*.[16]

Besides providing a type of spiritual rest and a day of worship, the Jewish Sabbath also had as a third object to furnish a day of relaxation for servants. That provision, Calvin tell us, is incidental. "Since this pertains to the rule of charity, it has not properly any place in the First Table, and is therefore added by Moses as an extrinsic advantage." [437]

That the rest for servants and other laborers provided for by the fourth commandment is an "extrinsic advantage" is a notion that Calvin has done little more than state elsewhere. Here, however, he discusses it fully. First, he maintains, there is no positive demand for six days of labor. That element is introduced into the precept to show the children of Israel indirectly how little of their time God actually required. "For he does not, as some have foolishly thought, make a demand here for six days' labor; but by His very kindness entices them to obedience, since He only claims a seventh part (of their time) for Himself." [438] The Lord wished to remind the Israelites that, apart from the Sabbath, they had more than enough time for all their own business.

This physical rest, he continues, is always to be seen in relation to the other two provisions of the commandment. Rest was given to servants and slaves so that they might have leisure to gather for public worship and to meditate upon the promise of the spiritual rest typified by their weekly resting. The "stranger within the gates" and even dumb animals were included in the Sabbath, not because they shared in the benefits that rest typified, but so that throughout the whole land, wherever one looked, nothing would mar or detract from the scene of complete rest. "Besides," as he observes, "if the very least liberty had been conceded to them (the Israelites), they would have done many things to evade the Law on their days of rest, by employing strangers and the cattle in their work." [439]

Finally, in commenting upon the phrase, "For in six days the Lord made," Calvin conjectures that hallowing the Sabbath probably existed before the giving of the Law at Sinai. That is so, he believes, because the prohibition of manna-gathering in

Exodus 16 seems to reflect that the Sabbath was a well-known custom. He also considers it "not credible"[17] that the Lord in revealing the rite of sacrifice to the Patriarchs did not also institute the weekly Sabbath.

•*Leviticus 19:30 (26:2)*
"Observe my Sabbaths and have reverence for my sanctuary. I am the Lord."

In commenting upon these parallel verses, Calvin stresses the indissoluble connection between the Sabbath and the worship of the tabernacle. The former is always the means to the latter. Rest without a purpose would have been a "mere mockery." "Nay more, after Moses has spoken of the rest, he seems to subjoin the reverencing of the sanctuary, as if it were the generic ordinance; so that the people might understand that all impediments were removed which are wont to withdraw them from the service of God." [442]

•*Exodus 23:12*
"Six days do your work, but on the seventh day you shall rest."

This statement, Calvin says, refers to the "incidental" use of the Sabbath, to what "is no inherent part of its original institution." [442] He gives no indication to what "its original institution" refers but goes on to reason that since giving rest to slaves and servants is an act of kindness, it belongs most properly to the second table. It is not inappropriately attached to the fourth commandment, however, because the recipients of rest are enabled thereby to better obey the command to worship and meditate.

•*Exodus 31:13-17*
Calvin's comments on these verses highlight a point already made in his exposition of Exodus 20:8-11. Keeping the Sabbath distinguished Israel and indicated its uniqueness among the other nations. By that sign the people were to know that God was their sanctifier. To fail to keep the Sabbath rest, therefore, was to

forfeit the blessing of sanctification. So the justice of the severity in punishing Sabbath-breakers can be appreciated. "Hence, again, we gather the dignity and excellency of the mystery, when God deemed an apparently light transgression of it worthy of death." [443]

The statement that Israel's Sabbath is "a perpetual covenant" (verse 16) involves certain difficulties, which Calvin anticipates and answers. To the objection that such language prohibits the view that Christ abrogated the Jewish Sabbath, he maintains that whatever the law speaks of as perpetual refers to the radically new state of affairs brought to pass by the advent of Christ. In other words, typical elements in God's eternal law ceased when the truth of all figures was manifested. At that time God's covenantal dealings assumed a new form that only has a place for the reality, not for the figure. So, he concludes, there is really nothing "which more completely confirms its [the Sabbath's] reality and substance than the abolition of its external use." [444] To cease keeping the type is not to disregard the Sabbath institution but to recognize its eternal reality. Those who refrain from the "external observance" of the Sabbath testify, by their restraint, that spiritual rest has become a reality.

Here we are given further insight into what we have already seen elsewhere. For Calvin, the questions of which the Christian day of rest is and how often it is to be kept are of relatively minor importance. To be preoccupied with these questions is to come dangerously close to reintroducing "external observance." The paramount requirement of the fourth commandment is that believers experience spiritual rest and exhibit the fruits of that experience in private meditation and public worship.

•*Exodus 23:10-11; Leviticus 25:1-8, 20*
These verses deal with the sabbatical year and the year of Jubilee. The point of Calvin's remarks is that the central feature of both these ceremonies was not the adjustments they made in Israel's internal affairs. Rather, they underscored the fundamental meaning of the weekly Sabbath by highlighting

that Israel was different from other peoples, that it had been separated from the other nations to be a peculiar and holy nation, and that God would be its sanctifier.

•Leviticus 23:4

Calvin's comments on this verse in its context note the affinity between the weekly Sabbath and the other feasts. All are holy convocations. Therefore, public worship must have been an integral element of Israel's Sabbath. "And surely it is plain that the Fourth Commandment had no other object or use except to exercise the people in the service of God." [455]

•Numbers 15:32-36

These verses record the celebrated incident of the man stoned to death for gathering sticks on the Sabbath. Here, too, Calvin insists, as we have already seen, that the reason for the severity of this punishment can only be appreciated in the light of the typical character of the Jewish Sabbath. "Moreover, by this severity God testified how much stress He laid upon the observance of the Sabbath. The reason of this has been elsewhere set forth,[18] viz., that by this mark and symbol He had separated His chosen people from heathen nations."[19]

He goes on to insist that it should not be concluded, since such a minute infraction was so severely punished, that keeping the Sabbath consisted in idleness and inactivity.

> But it must be borne in mind that the worship of God was not to consist in mere idleness and festivity; and therefore that what God enjoined respecting the seventh day had another object; not only that they should then employ themselves in meditating upon His works, but that, renouncing themselves and their own works, they should live unto God. [97]

•Numbers 28:9-10

Calvin observes that the doubling of the regular sacrifices on the Sabbath day was appropriate, "for it was reasonable that, as the seventh day was peculiarly dedicated to God, it should be exalted above other days by some extraordinary and distinctive mark."[20]

•*Psalm 92*

This psalm, in praise to the Lord for his mighty works, has for its superscription, "A Song for the Sabbath Day."

The appropriateness of that designation, Calvin says, is obvious. The Sabbath day has not been set aside for idleness, but to be devoted to worship acceptable to the Lord. That can only be accomplished by separating ourselves from our occupations and other distractions so that we may devote all our attention to meditating upon God's wonderful works. Rest from labor is always the means to the goal of meditation and worship. "The Psalmist then would teach us that the right observance of the Sabbath does not consist in idleness, as some absurdly imagine, but in the celebration of the Divine name."[21] Subsequently, he comments similarly on verse 4, "The Psalmist repeats the truth that the Sabbath was not prescribed as a day of idleness, but a season when we should collect our whole energies for meditation upon the works of God." [496]

Indicative of Calvin's understanding of the fourth commandment is his concern that, despite his insistence that the Jewish Sabbath is abrogated and the Christian is no longer bound by the number "seven," the meditation and worship that characterized Israel's celebration is equally demanded for the day of rest that believers now observe.

•*Isaiah 56:1-6*

Here, too, Calvin stresses that the Sabbath was not a ceremony of idleness, but was to be used for meditation and worship. "But we must view the Sabbath in connection with everything that attends it; for God does not rest satisfied with outward ceremony, or delight in our indolence, but demands from us earnest self-denial, that we may be entirely devoted to his service."[22] In fact, Calvin points out, in verse 2 the Sabbath is a synecdoche to include all religious exercise. In commenting on

"Sabbath" in verse 6, he repeats that the word is often used to comprehend the whole worship of God.

Verse 4 reveals the true meaning of Israel's Sabbath in yet another way, by closely conjoining it with the covenant. "With the 'keeping of the Sabbath,' he connects obedience and adherence to the 'covenant'; and hence we may readily infer that, when he spoke hitherto about the Sabbath, he had in view not idle ceremony but perfect holiness." [180]

•Isaiah 58:13-14

Because these verses are so often quoted in discussions about the Sabbath, Calvin's comments are particularly noteworthy.

He begins by noting that some people think the prophet is alluding to the external observance of the Sabbath. That he does not deny, but holds that "the meaning is far more extensive." What that meaning is becomes clear as he finds in Isaiah's words one of the most penetrating Old Testament analyses of the typical character of Israel's Sabbath.

The reference to "keeping your feet from breaking the Sabbath," he holds, does not so much have in view laws that forbade journeys on the Sabbath. Rather, this "walk" refers to a way of life. As the immediately following clauses bear out, it involves "doing," "calling," "knowing," "finding," and "speaking," – the entire scope of human conduct. To "turn away the foot from the Sabbath" is, freely and without restraint, to indulge one's sinful desires. Conversely, true Sabbath keeping does not consist in idleness one day each week, "but in true self-denial, so as to abstain from every act of injustice and wickedness, and from all lusts and wicked thoughts." Calvin continues:

> Certain classes of duties are again enumerated by him, by which he shows clearly that the true observation of the Sabbath consists in self-denial and thorough conversion .... For he contemplated something higher than an outward ceremony, that is indolence and repose, in which the Jews thought that the greatest holiness

consisted. On the contrary, he commanded the Jews to renounce the desires of the flesh, to give up their sinful inclinations, and to yield obedience to him; as no man can meditate on the heavenly life, unless he be dead to the world and to himself. Now, although the ceremony has been abolished, nevertheless the truth remains; because Christ died and rose again, so that we have a continual Sabbath; that is we are released from our works, that the Spirit of God may work mightily in us. [241-42]

This excerpt makes it clear that for Calvin the fourth commandment commanded Old Testament believers not only to spend each weekly Sabbath in worship and meditation on the promise of spiritual rest typified by the Sabbath, but also to practice such rest throughout every day cᶠ their lives. Reality and shadow existed side by side. How that was possible will become clearer when we discuss his remarks on Ezekiel 20:12.

•Isaiah 66:23

The contrast between what Calvin says here and in commenting on 58:13-14 is striking. Here he stresses the difference rather than the identity between the old and new covenants. This is another reminder of how important it is always to see any one statement about the Sabbath in the light of the whole of his teaching.

"There is only here a contrast between the Sabbath and festivals which were celebrated under the Law, and the perpetual Sabbath which we have at the present day." [439] Under the Law the Sabbaths and other festivals were observed at specific times and the offerings of sacrifices was carefully regulated. Under Christ, however, believers enjoy complete freedom of expression in worship. They are not bound by set times and days. Any time is appropriate for worship or offering up "spiritual sacrifices." The ceremonies of the Papists, accordingly, are no improvement on Judaism.

These remarks, we should also note, strongly confirm our conclusion that the *Institutes* identify the present spiritual rest of believers with eschatological rest, as being the same in principle. The *Institutes* quote this verse, clearly referring it to the rest that will not be perfected until the Last Day.[23] Here, however, everything said applies to the rest believers presently enjoy in Christ, with no mention of future eschatological rest.

•*Jeremiah 17:21-27*

The comments on this passage, first given in a series of lectures on Jeremiah, make several emphases by now familiar to us. Since these verses deal with Sabbath-breaking, Calvin stresses that keeping the Sabbath involved more for the Israelites than physical rest. "We now then perceive that the design as to the ancient people was, that they might know that they were to rest from all the works of the flesh."[24] The Sabbath was for meditation on rest from sin and for spiritual rest in God.

The Old Testament Sabbath, then, was a type, a "symbol of sanctification." "We learn especially from Paul that the Sabbath-day was enjoined in order that the people might look to Christ; for well known is the passage in Col. ii.16, where he says that the Sabbath as well as other rites were types of Christ to come, and that he was the substance of them." [381]

With the typical character of the Jewish Sabbath taken into consideration, the importance placed on keeping the day as well as the severity with which infractions were punished can be appreciated. Verses 24-25 indicate that the ultimate goal of Israel's aspirations, the perpetuity of the kingdom, was dependent on keeping the Sabbath day. Why that was so can be appreciated only when we recognize that "the end, which was spiritual, was connected with the outward rite." [386] Indispensable for the perpetuity of the kingdom was the righteousness of the people. Of that condition – that the people were called to holiness and sanctification – the Sabbath was a badge and symbol.

Finally, in the words of the prayer appended to this lecture, "thou dost not now prescribe to us one day on which we are to testify that we are sanctified by thee, but commandest us to observe a sacred rest through our whole life, so as to renounce ourselves and the world." [391] Such language, of course, is susceptible to the same sort of discussion we have already devoted to similar expressions of Calvin. It serves to remind us, again, that for him the questions of the particular day of rest and worship and the frequency of that day are not really essential to the present demands of the fourth commandment.

•*Ezekiel 20:12-20*

The content of these verses and the Jeremiah 17 passage is virtually the same. Not surprisingly, then, Calvin's remarks here are almost identical. He stresses again that true keeping of the Jewish Sabbath involved more than physical rest and cessation from labor. There is as well the closely related emphasis on seeing that Sabbath as a type of spiritual rest brought by Christ, a "symbol of sanctification."

His exposition here, however, has one unique feature. It is, so far as I can find, the only place where Calvin calls the Jewish Sabbath a sacrament. In discussing the typical function of the Sabbath, he notes that "it was only an outward symbol, and that it contains a spiritual mystery," and then adds, "It now follows, as I lately touched upon it, that the Sabbath was a sacrament, since it was a visible figure of an invisible grace."[25] A little later, commenting on verse 20, he says, "For we said that the Sabbath was a sacrament of regeneration." [311][26]

In ascertaining more precisely what these statements mean, it will help to be clear what they do not mean. First, they plainly refer only to the Old Testament Sabbath. As I will try to show, only because of what was unique to the Jewish Sabbath, its typical character, can Calvin call it a sacrament.

Secondly, these statements should in no way be seen as upsetting the two sacrament system for which the Reformers toiled. That the Lord's Day, along with baptism and the Lord's supper, is a sort of third sacrament is the farthest thing from Calvin's mind. Any difficulties in this respect may be easily resolved by taking into account how broadly he defines a "sacrament." "One may call it a testimony of divine grace toward us, confirmed by an outward sign, with mutual attestation of our piety toward him." And he adds that this definition does not differ from Augustine's teaching that a sacrament is "a visible form of an invisible grace."[27]

Calvin, then, apparently uses "sacrament" in a wider sense, as roughly equivalent to the phrase "means of grace." A sacrament is any external aid or stimulus to spiritual growth and development. In fact, we have explicit confirmation of his broader understanding of "sacrament." "The term 'sacrament,' ... embraces generally all those signs which God has ever enjoined upon men to render them more certain and confident of the truth of his promises."[28] He then mentions, among the Old Testament sacraments, not only circumcision, sacrifices, and rites of purification, but also such signs as the tree of life, the rainbow given to Noah, Gideon's fleece, and God's action in bringing the shadow on the sundial back ten degrees as a promise of safety to Hezekiah.

In a narrower sense, however, he does not include these signs and miraculous actions among the sacraments. The requirement for a sacrament in this sense is that it be a divinely instituted ceremony. The ceremonies of the Old Testament, circumcision and the sacrificial system, have been abolished by Christ. The sacraments (ceremonies) of the New Testament church, of which there are only two, baptism and the Lord's supper, have been instituted by Christ.[29]

With these qualifications in mind, the Ezekiel commentary plainly uses the term "sacrament" in the wider sense. The Jewish Sabbath was a sacrament, "since it was a visible figure of an invisible grace." Because the Sabbath typified the blessing of spiritual rest, it also functioned as a sacrament. Specifically, it was a "sacrament of regeneration."[30] For the Israelite who properly employed the time in worship and meditation upon spiritual rest, the Sabbath was a means and aid to regeneration, to enjoying sanctification and spiritual rest. When we recognize Calvin's use of "sacrament" in the wider sense, his remarks in this commentary present no difficulty. Rather, they are a natural consequence of all that he teaches elsewhere about the typical significance of the Jewish Sabbath.

•*Hosea 2:11*

Calvin's comment here is that Hosea prophesies that the Sabbath is among those things to be taken away from Israel because of their abuse of it, as well as other divinely-instituted ceremonies. Instead of using it properly for meditation and true worship, they had incorporated it into a "fallacious and empty form of religion in which they foolishly delighted."[31]

•*Matthew 12:1-8 (Mark 2:23-27; Luke 6:1-5)*

On the incident when the Pharisees accused Christ's disciples of breaking the fourth commandment because they picked ears of corn on the Sabbath, Calvin notes five arguments in Christ's rebuttal. All five are directed toward making the point that physical rest on the Sabbath was not an end in itself, but provided that the people "might be employed in true and spiritual rest; and next, that being free from all worldly occupations, they might be more at liberty to attend the holy assembly."[32]

First, Christ approves David's action of taking and then eating consecrated bread when no other food was available. If Christ pleads David's example, there was certainly nothing unlawful in the latter's actions. Therefore, if necessity permitted David's activity, it excuses others as well. This incident establishes the principle "that the ceremonies of the Law are not violated where there is no infringement of godliness." [48]

Second, on the Sabbath duties connected with the worship of the temple, such as circumcision and killing animals for sacrifice, were lawful. "Hence it follows, that the duties of piety are in no degree inconsistent with each other." [49] All the more, then, were the disciples free from guilt in their action, because they were engaged with Christ in the duties of founding the "true and spiritual temple."

Third, Christ reproves the Pharisees indirectly for not understanding the proper use of ceremonies. He charges them with Israel's age-old sin: rigorous observance of the minutest ceremonial detail, but without regard for the weightier matters of mercy and kindness. Throughout the entire Old Testament, God is unmistakably clear: he prefers mercy to sacrifice; whoever is occupied entirely with the latter and ignores the former, distorts the whole law.

This leads Calvin to anticipate a question. Why did God so strictly enjoin ceremonies in the law, since he appears to treat them with such indifference, as relatively unimportant? His answer provides the opportunity to make one of his favorite points. External rites, such as the observance of Sabbath rest, had no value in themselves. They were always a means to the end of worship and service of God; the apex of divine service is love and kindness toward neighbor. Sacrifice and mercy are inseparable.

Fourth, "For the Son of Man is Lord of the Sabbath." Christ has the authority to exempt his disciples from the obligation to observe the Sabbath, if he deems it necessary.

Fifth, "The Sabbath was made for man." Jesus informs the Pharisees that they have missed the whole point, if they think that the fourth commandment forbids the weary and hungry from a necessary journey for gathering food on the Sabbath. The day was set aside for man's benefit, not his destruction.

Calvin concludes by observing that, although Christ here asserts his authority over the Sabbath, we should recognize that at that time he was explaining its proper use, not abolishing it. "Though he asserted, a little before, that he is Lord of the Sabbath, yet the full time for its abolition was not yet come, because the veil of the temple was not yet rent." [51]

•*Matthew 12:9-13 (Mark 3:1-5; Luke 6:6-10)*
In all three Gospels this account of the incident when Christ was accused of Sabbath-breaking for healing a man with a withered hand immediately follows the verses just discussed. Accordingly, Calvin's comments on the two pericopes are much

the same, and I will take note only of those that did not appear in the previous exposition.

He seems to imply that ceremonies are not necessarily wrong in the Christian church; what must be guarded against is their abuse. "We learn also, that we ought to beware lest, by attaching undue importance to ceremonial observances, we allow other things to be neglected, which are of far higher value in the sight of God." [53] He goes on to state that the New Testament church must always emphasize the spiritual character of worship, even though human beings are "inclined to outward rites."

Just what ceremonies Calvin had in mind is difficult to say. Probably he is at least referring to baptism and the Lord's supper, for he considers them the ceremonies appointed by Christ.[33] That he admits the possibility of other ceremonies, ordained by the church, cannot be excluded, and even appears plausible in view of the general tone of his statement. That conclusion would be in keeping with his apparently mediating approach to the matter of feast days.[34]

He also points out that for the Pharisees to condemn Jesus for healing the man was, in effect, to condemn God, since the miracle was obviously a divine work. The Pharisees were again missing the point; God does not lay down a law that restrains his freedom of operation. They should have learned from the very graphic lesson Christ was teaching them; certain necessary works are lawful on the Sabbath. ·

•Luke 4:16

Here we come upon another one of those difficult statements where Calvin appears to contradict what he says elsewhere about the Sabbath. Christ entering the synagogue on the Sabbath day to read the Scriptures, he notes, shows the proper method of keeping the Sabbath. It was not a day of "indolent repose," but time to be spent in worship and meditation.

Paul, he continues, has included the Sabbath among those Old Testament types that have been abolished, but Christians must observe it in the same way as the Jews, at least in a certain respect: "the people must assemble to hear the word, to public prayers, and to other exercises of religion." And he concludes, "It was for this purpose that the Jewish Sabbath was succeeded by the Lord's Day."[35]

As far as I have been able to discover, here, in his comments on 1 Corinthians 16:2 (discussed below), and the reference in the *Institutes*[36] (noted earlier) are the only places where Calvin speaks of the Lord's Day as successor to the Old Testament Sabbath. The statement in the *Institutes*, we should recall, is immediately and drastically qualified by saying that he does not want to bind the church to the number seven.

Apparently, then, the statement here, along with its context, is subject to the same sort of qualification; conclusions should not be drawn in isolation from the rest of his teaching. In other words, he is maintaining that Christians as well as Jews have need of days devoted exclusively to private meditation and public worship, and that the weekly Lord's Day has been instituted in the church to meet that need.

He gives no indication how or by whose authority the Lord's Day succeeded the Sabbath. As I have already tried to show, in the *Institutes* he attributes that change to the early church fathers,[37] and there is no ground for assuming he has anything else in mind here. Similarly, only someone with the strongest predisposition to do so can maintain that Calvin is implying here that the "one-day-in-seven" principle is taught by the fourth commandment. Rather, we should conclude, he is again stating his approval of the weekly Lord's Day as a means for fulfilling obligations the fourth commandment makes on Christians.

•Luke 13:14

The synagogue rulers' annoyance at Jesus' choosing to heal the crippled woman on the Sabbath when he had six other days for doing so, prompts Calvin to remark that the power and mercy of God do not "lay asleep" on the Sabbath, but are "exerted chiefly on that day for the salvation of his people."[38] Works of mercy and kindness are lawful every day of the week.

•Luke 14:1-6

Calvin maintains that Jesus' purpose in healing the man afflicted with dropsy was not to abolish the Sabbath, as if he were now doing something previously unlawful on that day, but to correct Jewish superstition and to demonstrate what proper Sabbath observance involved. Sabbath rest is not an end in itself but has been given for a purpose. Mercy and kindness to man and beast are as appropriate on this day as any other. [162-64]

•John 5:1-18

Calvin's comments on this passage include a rather full statement of his views on the Sabbath question. By now most of what he says is familiar and need not detain us at any great length. His main point is that Jesus, by healing the lame man and giving him his bed to carry, shows the true meaning of the fourth commandment. He is not abolishing the Sabbath but freeing it from superstition.

Jeremiah 17:21, which forbids carrying any burden on the Sabbath day, provided the precedent for the Jews to challenge the recently healed man. Subsequently, Jesus shows, in effect, that this isolated Scripture is subject to qualification. The Sabbath day has not been given to hinder the works of God, but has been instituted for the sole purpose of promoting them. For the healed man to carry his bed was necessary, because it demonstrated the completeness of the miracle and the efficacy of the divine work involved.

Similarly, he continues, believers are called to consider God's work and to do what pleases him. For that purpose, the weekly day of rest was given to the Jews that they might devote the whole time exclusively to the Lord, leaving behind their own works for his. "Men are not conformed to God in this respect, that He ceased to work, but by abstaining from the troublesome actions of this world and aspiring to the heavenly rest."[39] In a very real sense, then, to rest in God is to do his work.

He points out further that Jesus' assertion that the Father continues to work does not at all contradict Genesis 2:2, which states that God has rested. Moses refers to God's cessation from the work of creation; Jesus speaks of his providential sustaining, maintaining, and undergirding of the creation. This equation of God's rest from creation with his works of providence became a standard emphasis in later Reformed thinking.[40]

•*John 7:22-23*
Here Jesus again defends his healing the lame man at Bethesda. His appeal is on the face of the text; as Calvin notes, the rite of circumcision was recognized by all the Jews as lawful on the Sabbath day. That sufficiently demonstrated "that the worship of the Sabbath is not violated by the works of God," [190] and that, therefore, Jesus was vindicated in making the man whole by his obviously divine exercise of power.

•*John 9:14-16*
This incident of healing the blind man on the Sabbath, similar to the healing at Bethesda, results in the same antagonistic reaction from the Jews. They again charge Jesus with Sabbath-breaking. Calvin's comments, accordingly, are similar:

> Besides, they had already been abundantly instructed by Christ, that the benefits which God bestows on man are not more inconsistent with the Sabbath than circumcision; and the words of the Law enjoin men to abstain from their own works only, and not from the work of God (Exod. xx. 8; xxiii. 12)." [375]

•*Acts 1:12*
Mention here of a Sabbath-day's journey (from Olivet to Jerusalem) prompts the observation, "There was no Sabbath-day's journey prescribed in the law, for the Lord doth in the law command them simply to rest upon the Sabbath day."[41] But because of the people's waywardness, the Sanhedrin found it necessary to make a ruling permitting any journey up to two miles in length on the Sabbath.

•*Acts 13:14*

Calvin's reflections on the detail that Paul and his companions entered the synagogue on the "day of the Sabbaths" provide implicit confirmation for concluding that he does not consider Christians bound by the language of the fourth commandment to keep a weekly day of rest. "Sabbaths" (the noun is plural in the Greek text) is used instead of the singular, he maintains, to show that for these men synagogue attendance was the rule, rather than the exception.[42] He says, "For they were wont to assemble themselves together upon the Sabbaths, lest their rest should be unprofitable and sluggish." [513]

This quotation strongly suggests that the Sabbath-keeping in view was a custom rather than an obligation. The governing verb used, translated "wont,"[43] always refers to what is usual, customary, habitual; it does not have normative force.

The objection is certainly in order that of itself the sentence quoted does not exclude the possibility that Calvin considered these men bound to observe the weekly Sabbath. That possibility is definitely ruled out, however, in the comments that immediately follow. He explains the relevance of the Sabbath institution for New Testament believers in terms by now familiar to us.

The Sabbath was a figure of spiritual rest. The truth of that figure has been manifested in Christ. Therefore, for believers the old figure has ceased to exist. But the Sabbath had another purpose. It provided a time for holy assemblies. The Jews, being free from their earthly labors, gathered for public worship. This second provision also concerns Christians. How? "So, even at this day we must use holy days [Sic et hodie feriis utendum est]; for we must therefore omit all things that we may the more freely serve God." [513]

This quotation seems to confirm our conclusion drawn from the earlier one that Christians are not bound by the fourth commandment to keep a specific day each week for rest and worship. Precisely what Calvin means by "holy days" is not at all clear. Certainly we should not conclude that he equates the

Lord's Day in all respects with other feast days appointed by the church. Whatever his attitude toward the latter, the former, as we have already seen, undoubtedly had a unique place in his thinking, distinct from other festivals.

At the same time, however, the Lord's Day must be included here among those "holy days" believers today "must use." The use of such days meets requirements that the fourth commandment still makes of believers. From this, two considerations may be drawn. First, "holy days" appears to be a generic term that includes Lord's Days. They are obviously not synonyms. The Latin ("feriis") makes that clearer than the English. If Calvin had meant the Lord's Day specifically, it is difficult to see why he did not say so. Consequently, since "holy days" embraces something more than Lord's Days, we can hardly maintain, in view of his consistent teaching elsewhere, that he considered them to be required by the fourth commandment. Second, since these "holy days" do not come under the provisions of the fourth commandment, the only reason that Christians "must use" them – and the context makes this clear – is to facilitate what he really does consider the present requirement of the commandment, namely the obligation to hold public assemblies for worship.[44]

All told, then, Calvin's point seems to be that Paul and the others with him recognized the obligation of the fourth commandment to assemble publicly for hearing God's word. For that they were accustomed to using the Jewish Sabbath and synagogue worship as a means for fulfilling this requirement, although the means itself was not prescribed by the commandment.

This conclusion is reinforced by his uniform teaching elsewhere. The coming of Christ released all believers, including Paul and his friends, from the obligation to keep the rest of the seventh day. As a sign of that freedom the church fathers chose the first day of the week for the Christian day of worship.[45] Therefore, for these men to enter the synagogue on the Jewish Sabbath was a purely voluntary act, demanded by no divine law.

Furthermore, to object that here he is only dealing with the attitude of these men toward the Jewish Sabbath, not whether or not the Lord's Day is required by the fourth commandment, misses the point. As the context makes clear, the duties of the fourth commandment are a central concern; the behavior of Paul and his friends is cited as an example of what the Christian's attitude, in part, toward the Sabbath institution should be: to observe days of rest and freedom from their worldly occupations, in order to be able to gather for public worship and to meditate privately without distraction. Keeping the Lord's Day helps to meet that obligation but, strictly speaking, is based not on the fourth commandment but the principle of "decency and order," and on the recognition that sinful human weakness precludes realizing the ideal of daily public worship.[46]

•*Acts 13:27; 13:44; 15:21; 16:13; 17:2; 18:4*
These verses all note occasions when Paul and others took part in synagogue worship on the Jewish Sabbath. Calvin's comments on them do not provide anything pertinent to this study.

•*Acts 20:7*
This verse, often cited in debates subsequent to Calvin's time to prove that the earliest Christians worshiped regularly on the first day of the week, elicits from him the equivocal comment, "Either doth he mean the first day of the week, which was next after the Sabbath, or else some certain Sabbath."[47] He then says that he favors the latter alternative because the Sabbath at that time was the customary day of assembly. Paul, he believes, waited until the first day of the week to make his departure, so that he could conveniently gather with the disciples on the final day of his stay with them.

•*Romans 14:5-6*
Though these verses are often cited to show that the Lord's Day, or any other day specially set aside for religious worship, has no

part in the life of the Christian, in commenting Calvin does not mention either the Sabbath or the Lord's Day. His concern, rather, is with superstitious observance and those who continue to celebrate typical ceremonies long after they have been abolished by Christ.[48]

•1 Corinthians 16:2

This verse, among those often cited to show that the New Testament church observed Sunday as its day of rest and worship, prompts Calvin to say, as in the case of Acts 20:7, that it refers rather to the Sabbath.

His remarks here are worth quoting at length because they state clearly the relation of Old Testament Sabbath to Lord's Day and so help to clarify earlier discussion in this study.

> Nor am I more inclined to admit the view taken by Chrysostom – that the term "Sabbath" is employed here to mean the "Lord's Day," (Rev. I. 10) for the probability is that the Apostles at the beginning, retained the day that was already in use, but that afterwards, constrained by the superstition of the Jews, they set aside that day, and substituted another. Now the "Lord's Day" was made choice of, chiefly because our Lord's resurrection put an end to the shadows of the law. Hence the day itself puts us in mind of our Christian liberty. We may, however, very readily infer from this passage, that believers have always had a certain day of rest from labor, not as if the worship of God consisted in idleness, but because it is of importance for common harmony, that a certain day should be appointed for holding sacred assemblies, as they cannot be held every day. For as to Paul's forbidding elsewhere (Gal. iv. 10) that any distinction should be made between one day and another, that must be understood to be with a view to religion, and not with a view to polity or external order.[49]

The accents here are unmistakable. The Sabbath was set aside by the leaders of the church (the apostles) in favor of the Lord's Day only after the contingency of Jewish superstition made that change necessary. Such a change, however, was only a political necessity. Out of a desire for common order, the Lord's Day was chosen, since sacred assemblies daily are impractical. The Lord's Day has been set apart solely for reasons of external order, not for any religious reason. Such reasons of piety or devotion, however, would necessarily have to belong to it, if Calvin believed that it had been set apart as a requirement of the fourth commandment. For him the Decalogue, in the last analysis, is nothing other than standards for piety and devotion. On the other hand, he can maintain, with complete consistency, that believers should always keep a day of rest in order to worship. Such observance was required of the Old Testament Jews; Christians freely choose to do so.

The passage just quoted is in complete harmony with and confirms Calvin's teaching in the *Institutes* and elsewhere concerning the present demand of the fourth commandment. Here, too, believers are called to experience perpetual spiritual rest and to express that rest in acts of worship and devotion. They voluntarily obligate themselves to the weekly Lord's Day so that they will be sure to have time for such worship and meditation.

•*Galatians 4:9-10*

Calvin's comments on this passage – one of the principal proof texts cited to show that the fourth commandment no longer demands the ceremonial observance of a day and that the typical function of the Sabbath is abolished – are of particular importance. However, since they present so many of the basic ideas already discussed repeatedly in this study, they need not detain us for any great length. Again, I will do little more than quote him at length in the hope that may clarify some of the conclusions we have already reached. Note how he stresses, once more, that observing the Christian day of rest is required not by reasons of religion or piety (that is, by the demands of God's law), but by concern for harmony and order in the church.

Of what nature, then, was the observation which Paul reproves? It was that which would bind the conscience, by religious considerations, as if it were necessary to the worship of God, and which, as he expresses it in the Epistle to the Romans, would make a distinction between one day and another. (Rom. xiv. 5)

When certain days are represented as holy in themselves, when one day is distinguished from another on religious grounds, when holy days [feriae] are reckoned a part of divine worship, then days are improperly observed. The Jewish Sabbath, new moons, and other festivals, were earnestly pressed by the false apostles, because they had been appointed by the law. When we, in the present age, make a distinction of days, we do not represent them as necessary, and thus lay a snare for conscience; we do not reckon one day to be more holy than another; we do not make days to be the same thing with religion and the worship of God; but merely attend to the preservation of order and harmony. The observance of days among us is a free service, and void of all superstition.[50]

Earlier in this study we noted that to a certain extent Calvin's reaction against Roman Catholic abuses motivated his approach to the Sabbath question.[51] But that motivation has not figured in the ensuing discussion, since he rarely mentions those with whom he disagrees. Here, however, caught up with concern over the harm to the gospel from false ceremonialism and the reintroduction of Judaism, his reaction to Catholicism surfaces, and the depth of his dread of its legalism is apparent.

And since that very description of impiety is now supported by Popery, what sort of Christ or what sort of gospel does it retain? So far as respects the bindings of consciences, they enforce the observance of days with not less severity than was done by Moses. They consider holidays, not less than the false prophets did, to be a part of the worship of God, and even connect with them the diabolical notion of merit. The Papists must therefore be held equally censurable with the false apostles; and with this additional aggravation, that while the former proposed to keep those days which had been appointed by the law of God, the latter enjoin days, rashly stamped with their own seal, to be observed as most holy. [125]

•*Colossians 2:16-17*

Perhaps no other passage was more important than this for establishing Calvin's basic contention that the typical character of the Jewish Sabbath, the sanctity inherent in any one day of the week, has vanished with the coming of Christ. Our own study has already noted, as even a quick glance at any of his writings on the Sabbath will show, how often he cites these verses as a proof text. His comments here, then, are of a basic character and present themes we have already meet with repeatedly. I limit myself to several quotations selected for the clarification they provide.

> He says, therefore, that it is not in the power of men to make us subject to the observance of rites which Christ has by his death abolished, and exempts us from their yoke, that we may not allow ourselves to be fettered by the laws which they have imposed.
>
> Such a mode of partition was suitable for the Jews, that they might celebrate religiously [sancte] the days that were appointed, by separating them from others. Among Christians, however, such a division has ceased.
>
> But some will say, "We still keep up some observance of days." I answer, that we do not by any means observe days, as though there were any sacredness in holidays [feriae], or as though it were not lawful to labor upon them, but that respect is paid to government and order – not to days.
>
> For the substance of those things which the ceremonies anciently prefigured is now presented before our eyes in Christ, inasmuch as he contains in himself everything that they marked out as future. Hence, the man that calls back the ceremonies into use, either buries the manifestation of Christ, or robs Christ of his excellence, and makes him in a manner void.[52]

•*Hebrews 4:7-10*

Calvin refers verse 8 ("if Joshua had given them rest") to both the Jewish Sabbath and Israel's dwelling in Canaan. His main point is that these verses teach the same goal for both the Old Testament believer and the New Testament Christian – spiritual rest, but that in each case the means to that end differs. The Sabbath and the bountiful life enjoyed in Canaan were types given to direct the Jews to the goal of true spiritual rest and prosperity. But Christians no longer make use of these types.

> And we may hence easily learn the difference between us and them; for though the same end is designed for both, yet they had, as added to them, external types to guide them; not so have we, nor have we indeed any need of them, for the naked truth itself is set before our eyes.[53]

The idea of spiritual rest he goes on to develop makes clear once more, when the heart of the Sabbath institution is in view, how little he is concerned with weekly days of rest or stated times for worship. On verse 9 he says, "He draws the conclusion, that there is a sabbathizing reserved for God's people, that is, a spiritual rest; to which God daily invites us." [98] Spiritual rest, he continues, means rest from our own sinful works – mortification of the flesh – so that God may work in us. In the final analysis, such rest is perfect conformity to and imitation of God. Though never fully realized until the perpetual Sabbath of heaven, it is, nonetheless, a rest that believers may enjoy in this life and toward which they must continually strive. "Thus believers enter it but on this condition, – that by running they may continually go forward." [99]

The question of the abrogation of the Jewish Sabbath also claims his attention here. He grants that it is not expressly mentioned but holds that the writer's main purpose in setting forth the true meaning of the Sabbath was to reclaim his readers from its superstitious observance. "But I doubt not that the Apostle designedly alluded to the Sabbath in order to reclaim the Jews from its external observance; for in no way could its abrogation be understood, except by knowledge of its spiritual design." [99] This abrogation, it should be noted again, is not the eradication of the Sabbath institution but the replacement of type with reality.

The closing comment on this passage is extremely instructive. It illustrates clearly how, when the core of the fourth commandment and the most ultimate consideration attaching to the Sabbath institution are in view, matters of public worship and days of rest become relatively insignificant for Calvin. "For he who understands that the main object of the precept was not external rest or earthly worship, immediately perceives, by looking on Christ, that the external rite was abolished by his coming; for when the body appears, the shadows immediately vanish away." [99]

Sermons

My 1962 thesis did not deal with two sermons on the fourth commandment. At that time I was unable to read them in the original (French) and unaware of existing English translations. Here I will discuss them for the sake of completeness but only briefly and largely by quoting excerpts. On examination, they reinforce but add little to the total picture of Calvin's views we have already obtained. They are, however, unique in opening an instructive window on how he preached on the Sabbath/Lord's Day issue, particularly, as we will see, on what may be called the "practical Sabbatarianism" they reveal. Part of a series on the ten commandments, within a larger series on Deuteronomy, they were preached in Geneva, not on the Lord's Day, interestingly, but on consecutive week days, Thursday, June 20, and Friday, June 21, 1555.[54]

The first of these two sermons is on 5:12-14 and develops two main points. First,

[t]he sabbath day [le jour du repos[55]] has been in part a figurative way for showing [une figure, en parte pour monstrer] that men cannot properly worship without dedicating themselves to him in such a way that they separate themselves from the world. Secondly, the sabbath day has existed as a ceremony whose purpose was to assist the people to assemble that they might hear the Law, call upon the name of God, and everything which concerns the spiritual order [police]. [97-98]

These two points, the reader may recognize, approximate the first two of the three main purposes of the fourth commandment, according to the *Institutes*[56] and the 1538 *Catechism*. The first of these is spiritual rest, of which "the sabbath day was a shadow under the Law until the coming of our Lord Jesus Christ to represent that God requires men to rest from all their own works, which is what I have been saying in a word: that we must mortify our nature if we hope to be in conformity to God." [98]

Spiritual rest is developed at some length and in a manner that reinforces its comprehensive sweep. Understandably, given the homiletical setting, the accent falls on "how this observation [concerning the rest in view in the fourth commandment] is applicable to us today." [101] Here, as elsewhere as we have seen, a controlling assumption is the permanent relevance of the Sabbath because of concern for it in one of the ten commandments.

> For if we take the Law of God in itself, we shall have a perpetual norm of justice. And certainly under the ten commandments God willed to give us a norm that would abide forever. Therefore we must not imagine that what Moses has recounted concerning the sabbath day is superfluous to us, not that the figure lives on, but we have its truth. [102-03]

Now that the ceremonial, shadowy aspect, the "ancient servitude" [101] of observing each seventh day, has ceased because it has been fulfilled in Christ, it has become clear (as was true already in the Old Testament) that spiritual rest is the concern not of just one day of the week but every day of our lives. As the Old Testament weekly Sabbath was a sign that God was the sanctifier of Israel, so spiritual rest, the reality, includes sanctification in its entirety. A couple of longer quotes suffice to amplify this point.

> Thus to return to our situation, seeing that today we do not have this rigid figure and that God has given us great liberty, which has been acquired by us through the death and passion of our Lord

Jesus Christ, let us learn to dedicate ourselves to him with solicitude, and to recognize (as I have already touched on) that we shall have to labor hard in everything else, that it will amount to nothing unless our affections are held in check, unless we go to the trouble of renouncing all our thoughts and desires in such a way that God only governs us, and that we solemnly declare that we ask only to rest in him. And for that reason God suggests himself as an example. For he was not content to command men to rest, but he showed the way. For after having created the world and all that it contains, he rested, not because he had to, or was in need of rest, rather its purpose was to invite us to contemplate his works that we might concentrate on them and nevertheless conform ourselves to him. Do we therefore wish to keep the spiritual rest? Everything, then, that is said about God desisting from his works also applies to us, for we must so conduct ourselves as to cease doing whatever seems good to us and what our nature craves. [104-05]

Now, in the light of this, we are admonished with respect to two things: the one is to be displeased with ourselves and always to grieve, although it seems to us we have gone to great lengths to subject ourselves to our God; nevertheless, let us recognize that we are always on the road and that of necessity there is much that is required and commanded in the Law that must be accomplished by us. It serves, accordingly, as a way of humbling us, seeing that God will always find so much more to command in us with respect to his service and the fact that we are nowhere near [fulfilling] the requirements of this spiritual rest. Now all of this provides us with an opportunity for our humiliation and sighing in true repentance; also, on the other hand, we must be that much more moved and excited to take advantage of the situation once we see [it]. How is that? It is true that God has granted me the grace to be willing to serve him, but how do I go about the latter? Alas, I am still far from attaining it. Thus, once we grasp that, will it not make our own endeavor more imperative? Thus in detesting the evil which is in us, let us be so much more inspired to profit continually in their [sic⁵⁷] rest, and to make progress in it, and for each of us daily to call ourself to account. Thus that is how God, after having given us an opportunity for humbling us [sic⁵⁸] throughout our life, shows us that we must be zealous to correct our vices and increasingly to mortify our flesh, that we might realize that it is not enough for our old man to be crucified in part, rather we must be entirely buried with Christ .... That is what is meant by the seventh day which is mentioned here. [107-08]

The second main point of the sermon "emphasizes that the sabbath day was a civil order for training the faithful in the service of God." [108] Specifically, this order set apart the weekly Sabbath for public worship. In that respect, "it applies as much to us as to the ancient people." He develops this applicability along lines already familiar to us. "If we were as ardent in the service of God as we should be .... " [108], then this imposed order would be unnecessary; we would assembly ourselves for worship, "... without a written law ... morning and evening...." But because we are beset with the same "weakness" as the Jews, the order still applies. [109]

As elsewhere throughout his writings, he makes clear that the order, required today by the fourth commandment, is not the seventh day or even one day in seven [111]. Appropriately, in view of Christ's resurrection, "which has delivered us from all bondage to the Law .... " "we" have changed the day for public worship to Sunday.[59] But it could be "Monday or any other day of the week." Ideally, gathering for worship "ought to be done every day ...." His own judgment is that "in any event, we ought to observe this order of having some day of the week, whether one or two." "But," he adds immediately, "all of that can be left up to the liberty of Christians."[60]

As part of his second point, Calvin exposes the poverty of the notion that the Sabbath day rest is for physical inactivity "but not involving anything else." [109] In doing so, he reveals, at some length, what may be fairly called his "practical Sabbatarianism." "If we turn Sunday into a day for living it up, for our sport and pleasure,[61] indeed how will God be honored in that?" And a little farther on, obviously confronting a perceived problem in Geneva at that time, he continues:

Now let us consider whether those who call themselves Christians require of themselves what they should. There is a large group which thinks that Sunday exists for the purpose of enabling them to attend to their own affairs and who reserve this day for that [purpose] as if there were no others throughout the week for deliberating their business. For though the bell tolls the sermon, they seem only to have time for their own affairs and for one thing and another. The rest glut themselves and are shut up in their houses because they do not dare display a manifest scorn on the streets; in any case, Sunday is nothing more than a retreat for them in which they stand aloof from the church of God.... But as everything is profaned, we see that the majority hardly care about the usage of this day which has been instituted in order that we might withdraw from all earthly anxieties, from all business affairs, to the end that we might surrender everything to God. [109-10]

"Moreover," he immediately adds,

let us realize that it is not only for coming to the sermon that the day of Sunday is instituted, but in order that we might devote all the rest of the time to praising God.... Thus we ought to observe Sunday as if from a high tower in order that we might climb upon it to contemplate the works of God from afar, in a way in which we are neither impeded by nor occupied with anything else, so that we might be able to extend all our senses to recognize the benefits and favors with which he has enlarged us. [110]

When we have benefited from spending Sunday in this fashion, then "we will surrender to him all the rest of our time, ... we shall be induced to thank God on Monday and all the rest of the week." But when, by not so using Sunday, people "profane ... the holy order ..., why should they be astonished if all the rest of the week is degraded?" [110]

And in the closing sentences of the sermon,

In addition we have the external order – insofar as it applies to us – which exists for the purpose of enabling us to set aside our affairs and earthly business in order that, abstaining from everything else, we might meditate on the works of God and be trained to recognize the favors which God bestows on us.... And when we have spent

Sunday in praising and glorifying the Name of God and in meditating on his works, then, throughout the rest of the week, we should show that we have benefited from it. [113]

Here Calvin shows himself, despite undeniable and decided differences in theological rationale for observing the Lord's Day, to be remarkably close, in practice, to later Puritan views, like those given confessional status in the *Westminster Standards*.[62]

The second of the two sermons, on Deuteronomy 5:13-15, opens with a lengthy paragraph, summarizing the first sermon, and, for the most part, continues by further elaborating spiritual rest and the proper use of Sunday, dealt with the previous day. Accordingly, I limit myself to several related matters addressed here but not in the first sermon.

Considerable attention at the outset is focussed on the clause, "you shall work six days" (v. 13). Reminiscent of what he writes elsewhere, "This must not be interpreted to mean that God commands us to work." [116] Our responsibility for daily work and to be industrious is amply clear on other biblical grounds, and, anyway, since the Fall, "the work in which men are now engaged is a punishment for sin." Rather, all told, "this statement about working six days was not given as a commandment, but it is rather a permission which God gives in order to reproach men for their ingratitude, unless, as he has indicated, they observe the sabbath day and keep it holy." [117] Again, "If men were able on their own strength to fulfill the Law, he would have said to them: 'Work!' But on the contrary he said: 'Rest in order that God might work.'" [118]

The phrase "... nor any of your animals, nor the alien within your gates, ..." (v. 14), prompts a line of reflection relevant to spiritual rest. Animals are obviously not "participants in that spiritual rest which we discussed earlier." [120] Nor is the Sabbath, a sign that God sanctifies his people, for "pagans and unbelievers; he does not sanctify them." [119] Why, then, is that sign even "extended to [cover] cattle and asses?" That happened that men might have a reminder before their eyes in order to be that much more moved. Therefore this Sacrament was not addressed to beasts ..., but ... to men who must keep it for their [own] benefit. ... it was in order that the Jews, seeing their stables closed, might understand. And what were they to understand? [That] God sets in our midst before our eyes even dumb animals as a sign and visible sacrament. And their purpose is that, for our part, we might be that much more retained for God's service, knowing that we would be violating the entire Law if we did not think of that which forms the principal part of all our life, which is, that we learn to denounce ourselves and no longer follow our [own] appetites, or reason, or wisdom. For our God should govern us. [119-20]

Interestingly, Calvin goes on to relate directly the ground, "you were slaves in Egypt and the Lord your God brought you out of there ..." (v. 15) to the command "that your manservant and maidservant may rest, as you do" (v. 14). He develops this tie at considerable length by addressing the apparent difficulty that the first table of the law is concerned with the worship and service of God, not with love and kindness toward others, the concern of the second table. Since the fourth commandment "is contained in the first table, it follows that it belongs to the spiritual service of God and that it is pointedly not a question about the charity which we owe our neighbors"; [122] in itself, the command that slaves be given respite rests on a consideration that is "only accessory." [121]

"Why then is it mentioned here?" [122] The answer lies in the "superabundant day of rest" which this respite, along with rest for animals, achieves. That "superabundance" [123], he goes on in some detail, highlights just how comprehensive spiritual rest is (to be) – the complete gratuity of our redemption from sin and the full totality of our being set apart unreservedly for the service of God.

At the same time, Calvin does not simply dismiss rest for slaves, because of its strictly ancillary aspect here, as irrelevant or unimportant. To the contrary, he challenges the congregation, especially the rich and powerful, and at some length, to be compassionate and benevolent toward those under authority or in poverty. In doing so, he gives this responsibility to "fulfill a fatherly function" the deepest and most enduring basis, one that is not tied to his particular time and circumstances but is valid in every cultural setting:

> But in spite of any [right of] superiority which might exist, it is essential that we always arrive at this point: that we are united together in one flesh as we are all made in the image of God. If we believe that those who are descended of Adam's race are our flesh and our bone, ought that not make us subject to humanity, though we behave like savage beasts toward each other? .... But there is still more: that is that the image of God is engraved in all men. Therefore not only do I despise my [own] flesh whenever I oppress anyone, but to my fullest capacity I violate the image of God. [126]

And he also points out to the congregation how essential it is for them, as God's redeemed people, in their relationships with others, always to remember, in the language of the commandment (v. 15), "that they were like poor slaves in the land of Egypt." [127]

Finally, toward the close of the sermon, Calvin reflects at considerable length on the commandment's inclusion of the alien, that is, those outside the covenant community. Earlier, as we noted above, he had already said that the Sabbath is not for the benefit of "pagans and unbelievers." [119] And now he observes, "Thus it seems that God profanes the Sacrament when he makes it apply to unbelievers and to those who are not circumcised as a sign of the covenant, to those who possessed neither the Law or the promises." [129]

The resolution to this apparent difficulty is to recognize that what God says about the alien "always applies to the people whom he chose and adopted." What is that application? how is it that "this [commandment] must serve us today"? [129] The answer: "... its purpose is to show us that vices must not be permitted in a people who make a Christian confession, so much so that they have to be punished even among those who are only passing through."[63]

Christians have this responsibility, involving the power of the civil government ("those who hold the sword of justice in hand, who control the government in this life," 130), because God's honor and the safety of his people are at stake. This duty is developed broadly, with the perversion of worship and other blasphemies by "papists and others" primarily in view, though it is unclear, and nothing is said explicitly about, whether Sunday observance is to be enforced on resident unbelievers. In his closing words on this matter:

> Therefore seeing that foreigners have been prohibited from doing anything that is contrary to the worship of God, let us understand that we have been doubly commanded to walk in all solicitude and in such humility and sobriety that foreigners may be convinced that it is in good conscience and without hypocrisy that we want God to be honored and that we cannot allow anyone to bring opprobrium to his majesty and glory. [131]

The sermon as a whole ends by accenting that the fourth commandment has enduring meaning for the church:

> Consequently this is what we have to emphasize in this text if today we want to keep what was commanded of the Jews, as by right in truth and substance it belongs to us. Thus in the same way that our Lord of old delivered his people from Egypt, so today he has delivered us from the pit of hell, and reclaimed us from eternal death, and the abyss of flames into which we had plunged, in order to gather us into his heavenly Kingdom, for he has purchased us through the blood of his beloved Son, our Lord Jesus Christ. [131-32]

References

1. Dates for the Latin originals of the commentaries examined will be given [in brackets] in the footnote for the initial citation of each; these dates are taken from the "Chronological index of Calvin's Writings" in de Greef, *The Writings of John Calvin*, pp. 237-41.

2. See above, pp. 24-25.

3. *Institutes*, 1:400 (2:8:34).

4. *Commentaries on Genesis*, 1 (trans. J. King; Grand Rapids: Eerdmans, 1948 [1554, 1563]): 106. Unless he explicitly indicates otherwise, his remarks concern the day of rest his readers (are to) observe.

5. "septimus quisque dies" (CO, 23: 33).

6. The validity of this assertion as well as of the observations that follow are best evaluated by a careful reading of Calvin's exposition.

7. Cf. *Institutes*, 1: 398 (2:8:32); see above, pp. 37-38.

8. This facet of Calvin's exegesis, as far as I can see, is missed and so not wrestled with by Primus (*Holy Time*, p. 127, n. 8 ["Calvin and the Puritan Sabbath," p. 65, n. 103]), in criticizing the "one-day-in seven" assessment of Kuyper and Praamsma (and mistakenly attributed to me). His observation that "they fail to note the significance of Calvin's emphasis on one day in seven as the *minimum* [his emphasis] for worship," is gratuitous so far as Calvin's exegesis of Genesis 2:3 is concerned and so does not address the problem of contradiction that concerns them.

9. *Institutes*, 1: 400 (2:8:34, second paragraph), quoted above, p. 43.

10. *Institutes*, 1: 398-399 (2:8:33).

11. *Institutes*, 1: 396-97 (2:8:30-31).

12. See above, pp. 45-47, 48.

13. *Commentaries on the Four Last Books of Moses*, 2 (trans. C. W. Bingham; Grand Rapids: Eerdmans, 1950 [1563]): 433.

14. Clearly, from the immediate context, in the latter part of this quotation Calvin meant to write "any other view than" (not "no other view than"). The problem here is not in the translation but the original. The Latin reads: "... non alio respectu quam ut quietam suam ponerent in Dei cultu" (CO, 24: 577). Calvin's own French translation (1564), intended, in part, to correct errors in the Latin edition (de Greef, *The Writings of John Calvin*, p. 106), has the same sense: "... sans autre regard que servir à Dieu en se reposant" (as cited in a footnote in the English translation; I was unable to consult the French edition).

15. 1: 396-97 (2:8:30-31).

16. 1: 398 (2:8:32). We should recall here that in the *Institutes*, although Calvin seems to teach that neither the particular day of Christian rest and worship nor the frequency of that day are stipulated by the fourth commandment, he cannot imagine a situation in which

the observance of a periodic day of rest would not exist and, for himself, prefers the weekly Lord's Day.

17. "... credibile non est ..." (CO, 24: 581). The assessment of Primus (*Holy Time*, p.126 ["Calvin and the Puritan Sabbath," p. 64]: "Calvin [rather] tentatively offers this possibility: ....") weakens Calvin's assertion.

18. *Commentaries on the Last Four Books of Moses*, 2: 434-35; see above, p. 82.

19. *Commentaries on the Last Four Books of Moses*, 4: 97.

20. *Commentaries on the Last Four Books of Moses*, 2: 301.

21. *Commentary on the Book of Psalms* (trans. J. Anderson; Grand Rapids: Eerdmans, 1949 [1557]), p. 493.

22. *Commentary on the Book of the Prophet Isaiah*, 4 (trans. W. Pringle; Grand Rapids: Eerdmans, 1948 [1551, 1559]): 177-78.

23. 1: 396 (2:8:30).

24. *Commentaries on the Book of the Prophet Jeremiah and the Lamentations*, 2 (trans. J. Owen; Grand Rapids: Eerdmans, 1950 [1563]): 391.

25. *Commentaries on the Book of the Prophet Ezekiel*, 2 (trans. T. Myers; Grand Rapids: Eerdmans, 1948): 302; "Iam sequitur, ut nuper attigi, sabbathum fuisse sacramentum, quia visibilis fuit gratiae invisibilis figura" (CO, 40: 485). This commentary, one of Calvin's last works, is a collection of lectures (on the first 20 chapters) given in the winter of 1563-1564 and was first published posthumously in 1565.

26. "Diximus enim sabbatum fuisse sacramentum regenerationis" (CO, 40: 492).

27. *Institutes*, 2: 1277 (4:14:1).

28. *Institutes*, 2: 1294 (4:14:18).

29. Cf. *Institutes*, 2: 1295-1297 (4:14:19-20).

30. Calvin can call the Sabbath a sacrament of "regeneration," while elsewhere he consistently refers to it as a figure or type of "sanctification," because he understands the former in a wider sense (than has subsequently become standard, at least in Reformed theology), virtually equivalent to the latter; cf., e.g., *Institutes*, book 3, chapters 3-10.

31. *Commentaries on the Twelve Minor Prophets*, 1 (trans. J.

Owen; Grand Rapids: Eerdmans, 1950 [1559]): 96.

32. *Commentary on a Harmony of the Evangelists*, 2 (trans. W. Pringle; Grand Rapids: Eerdmans, 1949 [1555]): 47.

33. Cf. *Institutes*, 2: 1295-96 (4:14:19).

34. See chap. 2, n. 41.

35. *Commentary on a Harmony of the Evangelists*, 1: 227.

36. 1: 399 (2:8:34).

37. Chap. 2, pp. 41-42.

38. *Commentary on a Harmony of the Evangelists*, 2: 156.

39. *Commentary on the Gospel According to John*, 1 (trans. W. Pringle; Grand Rapids: Eerdmans, 1949 [1553]): 196.

40. Cf., e.g., Geesink, *Gereformeerde Ethiek*, 1: 347; Kuyper, *Tractaat van de Sabbath*, pp. 13-15.

41. *Commentary upon the Acts of the Apostles*, 1 (trans. H. Beveridge; Grand Rapids: Eerdmans, 1949 [1552]): 55.

42. Whether or not this exegesis is correct is not our concern here.

43. "Solebant" (CO, 48: 287).

44. Even if "holy days" were a synonym for Lord's Days, the most that could be proved from this statement is that Christians have an obligation to keep the Lord's Day. The ground for that obligation would still not be given. Moreover, the freedom of these men in choosing for rest and worship that day of the week (the Jewish Sabbath) which they were no longer obligated to keep since the Resurrection, cannot be suppressed, no matter how one interprets Calvin here.

45. *Institutes*, 1: 399-400 (2:8:34).

46. *Institutes*, 1: 398 (2:8:32).

47. *Commentary on the Acts of the Apostles*, 2: 235.

48. *Commentaries on the Epistle of Paul the Apostle to the Romans* (trans. J. Owen; Grand Rapids: Eerdmans, 1947 [1540]): 496-99.

49. *Commentary on the First Epistle of Paul the Apostle to the Corinthians*, 2 (trans. J. Pringle; Grand Rapids: Eerdmans, 1948 [1546]): 68-69.

50. *Commentaries on the Epistles of Paul to the Galatians and Ephesians* (trans. W. Pringle; Grand Rapids: Eerdmans, 1948 [1548]), p. 124 (emphasis added). Note that the obviously generic usage of "holy days" (feriae) here confirms our conclusion that he

uses it generically in his remarks on Acts 13:14; see above, p. 101.

51. See above, chap. 1, pp. 14-20.

52. *Commentaries on the Epistles of Paul the Apostle to the Philippians, Colossians, and Thessalonians* (trans. J. Pringle; Grand Rapids: Eerdmans, 1948), pp. 191-93 (CO, 52 [CR, 80]: 110); the original of the Colossians commentary first appeared in 1548.

53. *Commentaries on the Epistle to the Hebrews* (trans. J. Owen; Grand Rapids: Eerdmans, 1949 [1549]), pp. 97-98.

54. *John Calvin's Sermons on the Ten Commandments* (edited and translated by B. Farley; Grand Rapids: Baker, 1980) pp. 97-113, 115-32 (French original, CO, 26: 283-95, 295-307). Farley designates these "The Fifth Sermon," and "The Sixth Sermon," in the light of editorial references to their classification in a subsequent (1562) edition (CO, 26: 283, n. 1, 295, n. 1); in the text they are entitled "fourth" and "fifth" ("Le Quatrième Sermon sur le Chap. V (v. 12-14)," "Le Cinquième Sermon sur le Chap. V (v. 13-15)." In the (London, 1583) translation of A. Goulding they are sermons 34 and 35 (*The Sermons of M. Iohn Calvin upon ... Deuteronomie*, 1 [Ann Arbor: University Microfilms, 1981]: 200-05, 206-12); see also the survey and analysis of these sermons in Primus, *Holy Time*, pp. 123, 128-32 (with slight differences, "Calvin and the Puritan Sabbath," pp. 61, 63, 65, 66-72).

55. "the day of rest." Throughout, unless I have missed it, Calvin does not use "Sabbath," even when referring to the Old Testament Sabbath, although elsewhere, in the 1560 French edition of the *Institutes* (CO, 3: 446ff.), he uses it interchangeably with "le jour du repos."

56. 1: 395 (2:8:28), 400 (2:8:34).

57. "this" ("en ce repos," CO, 26: 291).

58. "ourselves" ("nous" – surely reflexive here).

59. "le Dimanche" (which derives from the Latin, "dies Dominicum," "the Lord's Day"), here and elsewhere throughout this sermon, rather than the more explicit "le jour du Seigneur"; likewise in the French edition of the *Institutes* (CO, 3: 449-52 [2:8:33-34]).

60. This passage is yet another that makes it difficult to sustain the contention that, just a year earlier, in his Genesis commentary, he advocates the "one day in seven" principle; see above, pp. 73-81.

61. "... à faire bonne chere, à nous iouer, et aller à l'esbat ..." (CO, 26:292).

62. Among more recent scholarship, this practical continuity, though perhaps minimized, is recognized, for one, by Primus, *Holy Time*, p, 134 ["Calvin and the Puritan Sabbath," pp. 73-74].

63. Farley (n. 100) surmises a reference here to the arrest and eventual execution of Michael Servetus in Geneva two years earlier.

Chapter 4

Other Reformers and Reformation Creeds

With our lengthy survey of Calvin's views completed, the purpose of this chapter is to provide some further perspective on them by briefly noting the immediate historical context provided by the views of other Reformers and contemporary evangelical creeds on the Sabbath/Lord's Day question. Let me stress that I intend little more than a quick sketch, which I trust is reliable as far as it goes. This will consist largely of excerpts, with minimal discussion.[1]

Martin Luther (1483-1546)

1. *Treatise on Good Works* (1520)
The work is an exposition of the ten commandments. The comments on the third commandment[2] begin by showing its relation to the first two.

> In the First Commandment is prescribed our heart's attitude toward God in thoughts; in the Second, that of our mouth in words, in this Third is prescribed our attitude toward God in works; and it is the first and right table of Moses on which these three commandments are written, and they govern man on the right side, namely, in the things which concern God, and in which God has to do with man and man with God, without mediation of any creature.[3]

"The first works of this commandment," he continues, "are plain and outward, which we commonly call worship [Gottesdienst], such as going to mass, praying, and hearing a sermon on holy days." [222] A lengthy discussion of worship follows, indicating that he considers it the primary concern of the commandment.

He maintains, however, that the scope of what this precept requires involves much more than acts of worship. The commandment is grounded in the rest of God from his work of creation. "Therefore He commanded also that the seventh day should be kept holy and that we cease from our works which we do the other six days. This Sabbath has now been changed into Sunday, and the other days are called work-days; the Sunday is called rest-day or holiday or holy day." [240] He then expresses the desire that all church holidays be done away with, except Sunday, so that it might be used properly and more honest work done on other days.

"This rest of ceasing from labors is of two kinds, bodily and spiritual. For this reason this Commandment is also to be understood in two ways." [241] With this statement Luther introduces ideas subsequently reflected and more fully developed in Calvin. Bodily rest is only so that believers may have opportunity to gather in church for mass, prayers, and the reading of God's word. "This rest is indeed bodily and in Christendom no longer commanded by God, ... for they were of old a figure, but now the truth has been fulfilled, so that all days are holy days, ..., on the other hand, all days are work days." [241][4]

Yet Sunday is a practical necessity, ordained by the church out of concern for "imperfect laity and working people" so that they might have an opportunity to hear God's word. However, since priests and clergy are involved every day in celebrating mass, praying at all hours, and studying God's word, for them every day is holy and they have no need for a special day of rest. "For a day of rest is at present not necessary nor commanded except only for the teaching of God's word and prayer." [241]

This notion of spiritual rest is similar to that found in Calvin. "The spiritual rest which God particularly intends in this commandment, is this: that we not only cease from our labor and trade, but much more, that we let God alone work in us and that we do nothing of our own with all our powers." [241] The ensuing discussion makes clear by an abundant use of biblical idiom that spiritual rest is achieved by dying to self and mortifying the flesh, which is accomplished by meditating on God's word.

Finally, noteworthy is Luther's stating of the third commandment at the beginning of his exposition: "Thou shalt hallow the day of rest [Feiertage]." [222] How he justifies such freedom in handling the language of Scripture he does not indicate. Clearly, however, that rendering, if its legitimacy be granted, frees him from the difficulties attendant on saying that Sunday has replaced the seventh day Jewish Sabbath.

2. *On the Councils and the Churches* (1539)

That Luther considers Christians free from any obligation either to keep Sunday as the Lord's Day or even to observe a weekly day of rest becomes apparent when he opposes the myriads of festivals and holy days maintained by the Roman Catholic church.

> Nay, you say, Sunday must be held in honor because of Christ's resurrection, and it is called dies dominica, on that account, and Easter must be put on it, because Christ rose on the day after the Sabbath, which we now call Saturday. That is, indeed, an argument that moved them; but dies dominica does not mean Sunday, but "Lord's Day," and why could not any day on which Easter had come be called dies dominica, "the Lord's Day"? Is not Christmas also dies dominica, "the Lord's Day," i.e., the day on which the Lord's special act, His birth, was done, and yet it does not come, every year, on Sunday? It is called Christ's Day, i.e., the Lord's Day, even if it comes on Friday, for the reason that it has a fixed letter in the calendar, reckoned by the sun. In the same way, Easter, too, could have a fixed letter in the calendar, whether it came on Friday or Wednesday, as is the case with Christmas. That way we should be well rid of the law of Moses, with its March full moon.[5]

3. *Large Catechism* (1529)

Rather than having the usual question-and-answer format this catechism is in an exposition of the faith. The following excerpts are on the third (fourth) commandment, rendered, as in the *Treatise on Good Works*, "Thou shalt sanctify the holy day."

> In the Old Testament, God set apart the seventh day and appointed it for rest, commanding it to be kept holy above all other days. In point of outward observance, the commandment was given only to the Jews.
>
> Therefore, this commandment, in its literal, coarse [groben] meaning, is not for us Christians now. It is wholly an external matter, like the other ordinances of the Old Testament, which were bound to particular customs, persons, times, and places, from all which we are now set free through Christ.[6]

Sundays are kept, Luther continues, not because "intelligent and learned" Christians have need of them, but for the sake of the weak and ignorant. They are kept because of bodily necessity – nature demands periodic times for rest and recreation – but especially so that there might be time and opportunity for laborers to gather for worship.

> But these concerns, I say, are not so bound up with a particular time as they were among the Jews, when it had to be precisely this or that day, for one day in itself is no better than another, and worship should, indeed, be observed daily. But since the mass of people cannot attend to it daily, one day a week at least must be set apart for the purpose. Sunday was appointed for it in olden times, and we should not change the day. The Sabbath should be uniformly observed as to the day and so no disorder be caused by unnecessary innovations.
>
> Hence, the true office of these days is the office of the ministry of the Word, for the sake of the youth and the poor multitude. However, our celebration should not be so narrow as to forbid incidental and unavoidable work.
>
> And, indeed, we as Christians ought to consider all days holy and be occupied only with holy things, that is, with daily meditation on God's Word, carrying it in our hearts and upon our lips. [60-61]

Among other similarities to Calvin's views apparent in these statements is the view that the Lord's Day has a prudential and purely human origin, designed to accommodate sinful weakness that prohibits realizing the ideal of daily public worship.

4. *Lectures on Genesis* (1535)

Some of Luther's comments on Genesis 2:3 seem to contradict what he says elsewhere about the Sabbath, just as certain of Calvin's remarks on the same verse, as we have seen, appear to introduce self-contradiction.

Addressing God's sanctifying the seventh day, he says, "Therefore from the beginning of the world the Sabbath was intended for the worship of God."[7] That would indicate that Luther, like Calvin, held the Sabbath to be in some sense a creation ordinance.

Among apparently contradictory statements is the following, which seems to say that believers are still bound to keep the seventh day.

> Therefore although man lost his knowledge of God, nevertheless God wanted this command about sanctifying the Sabbath to remain in force. On the seventh day He wanted men to busy themselves both with His Word and with the other forms of worship established by Him, ... This is what the Sabbath, or the rest of God, means, on which [day] God speaks with us through His Word and we, in turn, speak with Him through prayer and faith. [80-81]

This statement should be viewed in the same way as Calvin's remarks on Genesis 2:3. Luther is hardly contradicting everything he says elsewhere about believers no longer being obligated by God's law to keep a weekly day of rest. Rather, he frames his remarks in the language of the Sabbath institution as originally given and expects his readers to understand them in terms of what that ordinance now requires, namely spiritual rest and its expression in worship, which should be a daily, perpetual concern.

5. *The Small Catechism* (1529)

This catechism was obviously designed for instructing young children and converts. The brevity and pointedness of its questions and answers have the advantage of enabling us to see the core of Luther's convictions on the matters he treats.

The third (fourth) commandment is stated, "Thou shalt keep holy the Sabbath day [Feiertage]." The question is then asked, "What does this mean?," followed by the answer: "We should so fear and love God as not to despise preaching and his Word, but deem it holy, and willingly hear and learn it."[8]

The primary requirement of this commandment, then, is involvement in God's Word, an involvement that naturally expresses itself in public worship where the element of preaching is prominent.[9]

This treatment, though brief, discloses a high degree of similarity between the views of Luther and Calvin on the Sabbath. Both consider it a creation ordinance, in that it is rooted in God's own rest at creation. Both agree that the Sabbath day commanded of Israel was a type of spiritual rest and that the obligation to keep a weekly day of rest ceased with the coming of Christ, at whose advent all types vanished. For both, the fourth commandment now requires believers to practice a perpetual spiritual rest from sin, a rest involving private meditation and public worship. Both look at the observance of the Lord's Day not as a requirement of the fourth commandment but as an expedient necessitated by human weakness that prohibits realizing the ideal of daily worship. Luther does seem to go beyond Calvin in flatly asserting that the clergy and other intelligent Christians have no need of the Lord's Day or any other day specially set aside for rest and worship. It is difficult to imagine Calvin envisioning any state of affairs where the Lord's Day would not be kept by all believers.

Zacharias Ursinus (1534-1583)

Ursinus is perhaps best known as co-author, with Caspar Olevianus, of the *Heidelberg Catechism*, which first appeared in 1563.[10] Here we will survey material from his lectures on the catechism, given in the years prior to 1577 while a member of the theological faculty at Heidelberg. These lectures were compiled and published posthumously, appearing in book form in 1591.[11]

Ursinus is often considered a third generation representative of the Reformation. Strictly speaking, however, he is a contemporary of Calvin. The *Heidelberg Catechism* appeared just a year before Calvin's death, and Ursinus' comments on it in the years immediately following. His views, then, are representative of the German Reformed branch of the Reformation at roughly the same time Calvin was active in Geneva.

Question 103 of the *Heidelberg Catechism* asks, "What doth God require in the fourth commandment?" The answer is,

> First, that the ministry of the gospel and the schools be maintained; and that I, especially on the Sabbath, that is,[12] on the day of rest, diligently frequent the Church of God, to hear his word, to use the sacraments, publicly to call upon the Lord, and contribute to the relief of the poor as becomes a Christian. Secondly, that all the days of my life I cease from my evil works, and yield myself to the Lord, to work by his Holy Spirit in me, and thus begin in this life the eternal Sabbath. [557]

Ursinus begins by commenting on the language of the commandment itself. There are two parts – "the one moral and perpetual, as that the Sabbath be kept holy; the other ceremonial and temporary, as that the seventh day be kept holy." [557]

The perpetual moral design is for the maintenance of public worship. Specifically, by this precept God intends to insure that: 1) he is publicly praised and worshiped; 2) the elect are confirmed in their faith by worship; 3) believers mutually strengthen each other in the gospel and their desire to do good works; 4) agreement in Christian doctrine and practice is preserved and maintained; and 5) the church is visible in the world, distinct from the rest of humanity.

> Inasmuch now as these reasons do not have respect to any particular time, but to all times and conditions of the church and world, it follows that God will always have the ministry of the church preserved and the use of these respected, so that the moral part of the commandment binds all men from the beginning to the end of the world, to observe some Sabbath, or to devote a certain portion of their time to sermons, public prayers, and the administration of the sacraments. [557][13]

The ceremonial part of the commandment, the seventh day Sabbath, is not perpetual. It was instituted at Sinai for the observance of Mosaic worship. It was also given as a sign of spiritual rest, "as a sacrament or type of the sanctification of the church by the Messiah. Hence the Sabbath, in so far as it has respect to the seventh day, together with other ceremonies and types, was fulfilled and abolished by the coming of the Messiah." [557-58] The example of God resting from his work of creation on the seventh day notwithstanding, Ursinus insists, the command to observe the Sabbath on the seventh day is still only ceremonial. The moral consideration to be drawn from God's example is that we should imitate him. In the final analysis, such imitation means, as in Calvin, rest from sin and meditation on God's works.

After discussing the language of the commandment,[14] Ursinus addresses certain questions relative to the Sabbath. The first asks, "What and how manifold is the Sabbath?"

In answering Ursinus introduces another distinction – between the internal and external Sabbath. The former corresponds to the moral, the latter to the ceremonial Sabbath.

The internal Sabbath is spiritual rest from sin. It involves meditating on God's works and obeying his laws. "Or we may define it more briefly as a ceasing from sin, and a giving of

ourselves to God to do such works as he requires from us." [562]
This internal Sabbath is to be kept perpetually in this life,
although it will not be perfectly realized until the Sabbath of the
life to come.

> The ceremonial or external Sabbath is a certain time set apart in the
> church for the preaching of the word and for the administration of
> the sacraments, or for the public worship of God, during which
> time there is a suspension or abstinence from all other works. [562]

This external Sabbath, in turn, has a dual character,
immediate and mediate. The immediate external Sabbath was
directly instituted by God for the Old Testament economy. It
included the weekly Sabbath, the new moons, and the Sabbatical
years. The mediate external Sabbath has been instituted by God
through the church for the New Testament economy.

> Or to express it more briefly, we may say that the ceremonial
> Sabbath is two-fold: the one belonging to the Old, the other to the
> New Testament. The old was restricted to the seventh day: its
> observance was necessary, and constituted the worship of God.
> The new depends upon the decision and appointment of the
> church, which for certain reasons has made choice of the first day
> of the week, which is to be observed for the sake of order, and not
> from any idea of necessity, as if this and no other were to be
> observed by the church. [562-63]

The notion of the Lord's Day as a "mediate, external
Sabbath" presents a problem. In this view, on the one hand, the
Lord's Day is instituted by God. On the other, the day is not
observed out of any necessity. It is difficult to see how he can
consider observing a divine institution unnecessary, particularly
when he has just said that it was necessary to observe the Old
Testament Sabbath because God had commanded it.

The solution to this problem likely lies in the idea that
institution of the Lord's Day by God is mediate, through the
church. I take that to mean that the Lord's Day, in contrast to the

Jewish Sabbath which was expressly commanded by God, was chosen by the early church out of a concern for order. God can be said to have instituted it only in the sense that the affairs and actions of the church are under his sovereign control.

This assessment seems confirmed by the answer to the next question raised, "In how far does the Sabbath belong to us?" The main point is that, although the ceremonial Sabbath of the seventh day has been abolished, it is still necessary for a certain time to be set apart in the church for preaching and publicly administering the sacraments.

> Yet we must not suppose that we are restricted or tied down either to Saturday, Wednesday, or any other day. The apostolic church, to distinguish itself from the Jewish synagogue, chose, in the exercise of the liberty conferred upon it by Christ, the first day of the week in the place of the seventh, because on that day the resurrection of Christ took place, by which the internal and spiritual Sabbath is begun in us. [563]

Clearly Ursinus does not consider observing the Lord's Day a universally binding divine commandment. I see no real progression or difference between Calvin and Ursinus on this matter.[15]

The rest of Ursinus' treatment need not detain us. He develops more fully some of the themes we have already noted, particularly those related to the proper use of the Lord's Day and the practical reasons for its institution, and, in a lengthy discussion, maintains, as the catechism answer itself does, that the ministry of the church is one of the basic concerns of the fourth commandment.

The Evangelical Creeds

The following excerpts from important sixteenth century evangelical creeds provide a broader representation of views on the Sabbath or Lord's Day contemporary more or less with Calvin.

1. *The Augsburg Confession* (1530)

What is then, to be thought of the Lord's Day, and of like rites of temples? Hereunto they [ours] answer, that it is lawful for Bishops or Pastors to make ordinances, whereby things may be done in order in the church; not that by them we may merit grace, or satisfy for sins, or that men's consciences should be bound to esteem them as necessary services, and think that they sin when they violate them, without the offense of others. So Paul ordained, "that women should cover their heads in the congregation" (I Cor. xi.6); "that the interpreters of Scripture should be heard in order in the church" (I Cor. xiv. 27), etc.

Such ordinances it behooveth the churches to keep for charity and quietness' sake, so that one offend not another that all things may be done in order, and without tumult in the churches (I Cor. xiv. 40 and Phil. ii. 14), but so that consciences be not burdened, so as to account them as things necessary to salvation, and think they sin when they violate them, without offense of others; as no one would say that a woman sins if she went into public with her head uncovered, provided it were without offense of men.

Such is the observation of the Lord's Day, of Easter, of Pentecost, and like holidays and rites. For they that think that the observation of the Lord's day was appointed by the authority of the Church, instead of the Sabbath, as necessary, are greatly deceived. The Scripture, which teacheth that all the Mosaical ceremonies can be omitted after the Gospel is revealed, has abrogated the Sabbath. And yet, because it was requisite to appoint a certain day, that the people might know when they ought to come together, it appears that the [Christian] Church did for that purpose appoint the Lord's Day: which for this cause also seemed to have been pleasing, that men might have an example of Christian liberty, and might know that the observation, neither of the Sabbath, nor of another day was of necessity.

There are certain marvelous disputations touching the changing of the law, and the ceremonies of the new law, and the change of the Sabbath: which all arose from the false persuasion, that there should be a service in the Church, like to the Levitical; and that Christ committed to the Apostles and Bishops the devising of new ceremonies which should be necessary to salvation. These errors crept into the Church, when the righteousness of faith was not plainly enough taught. Some dispute that the observation of the Lord's Day is not indeed of the law of God, but *as it were* of the law of God; and touching holidays, they prescribe how far it is lawful to work in them. What else are such disputations but snares for men's consciences? For though they seek to moderate traditions, yet the equity of them can never be perceived so long as the opinion of necessity remaineth; which must needs remain, where the righteousness of faith and Christian liberty are not known.[16]

2. *The Formula of Concord* (1576)

The *Formula*, a Lutheran confession, makes no reference to the Lord's Day. The following statements are among the affirmative propositions under Article 10, *Of Ecclesiastical Ceremonies*.

I. For the better taking away of this controversy we believe, teach, and confess, with unanimous consent, that ceremonies or ecclesiastical rites (such as in the Word of God are neither commanded nor forbidden, but have only been instituted for the sake of order and seemliness) are of themselves neither divine worship, nor even any part of divine worship. For it is written (Matt. xv. 9): "In vain they do worship me, teaching for doctrines the commandments of men."

II. We believe, teach, and confess that it is permitted to the Church of God anywhere on earth, and at whatever time, agreeably to occasion, to change such ceremonies, in such manner as is judged most useful to the Church of God and most suited to her edification.

V. We believe, teach, and confess that one Church ought not to condemn another because it observes more or less of external ceremonies, which the Lord has not instituted, provided only there be consent between them in doctrine and all the articles thereof, and in the true use of the sacraments. For so runneth the old and true saying: "Dissimilarity of fasting does not destroy similarity of faith."[17]

3. *The First Helvetic Confession* (1536)

Now we believe that holy assemblies ought to be conducted so that above all the word of God be proclaimed publicly to the general population daily, that the secret things of Scripture be searched out and explained by competent ministers daily; that the faith of the pious be cultivated by celebrating the holy Eucharist regularly, that prayers be pursued constantly for all necessary concerns of all men.[18]

4. *The Second Helvetic Confession* (1566)

This major confession of the Swiss Reformed church, authored by Heinrich Bullinger, has the added advantage of providing a statement of the personal views of this important Reformer.

Chapter 22, "Of Religious and Ecclesiastical Meetings," does not mention the Lord's Day. A major emphasis is that public worship has been integral to the life of the church since apostolic times and so should be practiced now. The only biblical principle cited as governing these assembles is Paul's injunction that all things be done decently and in order.

Chapter 24, "Of Holy Days, Fasts and the Choice of Foods," begins with the following statement on the necessity for stated times of worship:

Although religion is not bound to time, yet it cannot be properly cultivated and exercised without a proper distribution and arrangement of time. Every Church, therefore, chooses for itself a certain time for public prayers, and for the preaching of the Gospel, and for the celebration of the sacraments; and no one is permitted to overthrow this appointment of the Church at his own pleasure. For unless some due time and leisure is given for the outward exercise of religion, without doubt men would be drawn away from it by their own affairs.

And then continues concerning the Lord's Day:

Hence we see that in the ancient churches there were not only certain set hours in the week appointed for meetings, but that also the Lord's Day itself, ever since the apostles' time, was set aside for them and for a holy rest, a practice now rightly preserved by our Churches for the sake of worship and love.

In this connection we do not yield to the Jewish observance and to superstitions. For we do not believe that one day is any holier than another, or think that rest itself is acceptable to God. Moreover, we celebrate the Lord's Day and not the Sabbath as a free observance.[19]

5. *The French Confession of Faith* (1559)

29. As to the true Church, we believe that it should be governed according to the order established by our Lord Jesus Christ. That there should be pastors, overseers, and deacons, so that true doctrine may have its course, that errors may be construed and suppressed, and the poor and all who are in affliction may be helped in their necessities; and that assemblies may be held in the name of God, so that great and small may be edified.[20]

6. *The Belgic Confession* (1561), *The Scotch Confession of Faith* (1560), *The Thirty-nine Articles of the Church of England* (1562)

None of these confessions refers to the Sabbath or Lord's Day question.

The above excerpts, though fragmentary, permit certain observations. The Sabbath or Lord's Day question does not have a very significant place in these earliest evangelical creeds. For the most part they do not give it more than perfunctory treatment; in some cases it is not even mentioned.

Two differing explanations may be given for that attitude. Either the sixteenth century Reformation church was basically indifferent to observing the Lord's Day, or they were in such general agreement about keeping it that it was not among those controversial matters that warranted attention in their creeds.

The latter appears to be the more likely explanation. All the evidence points to the conclusion that in every major branch of the Reformation church the Lord's Day was highly regarded and universally observed.[21]

Only with passing time and, we may suggest, a noticeable waning of the zeal for God's word and worship that characterized the early generations of the Reformation did the Lord's Day fall into disuse, and the need for observing it become increasingly challenged.

The sometimes less than careful and faulty formulations of the earlier Reformers no doubt gave comfort and support to those in later generations who argued that the Lord's Day has no relation to the fourth commandment and may be employed primarily for physical rest and recreation. However, the Reformers' apparent indifference toward the Sabbath question is in fact a signal indication of their unquestioned acceptance of the Lord's Day as the Christian day of meditation and worship. That any right-thinking Christian would seriously challenge the propriety, even the practical necessity, of using it for those purposes scarcely entered their minds.

References

1. Cf. Bauckham, "Sabbath and Sunday in the Protestant Tradition," pp. 317-21.

2. Even after his break from Rome, Luther continued to employ the standard medieval method of numbering the commandments. That system combines what Calvin and most Protestants today consider the first and second commandments into one. The tenth commandment in the Protestant system is then divided into two, still giving the customary number of ten.

3. *Treatise on Good Works* (trans. W. Lambert; *Works of Martin Luther*, 1 (Philadelphia: A. J. Holman, 1915): 222.

4. The omissions in this quotation are excerpts from Colossians 2:16 and Isaiah 66:23, cited as proof.

5. *On the Councils and the Churches* (trans. C. Jacobs; *Works of Martin Luther*, 5, Philadelphia: A. J. Holman, 1931), p. 184.

6. *Large Catechism* (Minneapolis: Augsburg, 1935), p. 60.

7. *Lectures on Genesis, Chapters 1-5*, ed. J. Pelikan, *Luther's*

Works, 1 (trans. G. Schick; St. Louis: Concordia, 1958): 80.

8. *Luther's Small Catechism*, in P. Schaff, *The Creeds of Christendom*, 3 (New York: Harper & Brothers, 1877): 74-75.

9. Cf. "Sunday," *What Luther Says*, 3 (compiled by E. Plass; Saint Louis: Concordia, 1959): 1328-31, for further excerpts from Luther's writings.

10. Schaff, *Creeds*, 1: 533-35.

11. *Commentary on the Heidelberg Catechism* (trans. G. Willard; Phillipsburg: Presbyterian and Reformed, 1985), p. xix.

12. The words "on the Sabbath, that is," were not part of the German original ["am Feiertag"], but were added in the Dutch translation of 1566 and have been retained in most official English translations.

13. Note that this moral, universally binding part of the commandment does not specify that a particular day of the week be set apart, nor does it demand the "one-in-seven" principle.

14. I have limited myself to noting briefly only the salient features of that discussion.

15. Fairbairn (*Typology of Scripture*, 2: 453) argues, partially on the basis of this statement, that Ursinus held to the "one-day-in-seven" principle. In the same context, however, he agrees with one of the basic conclusions of this study; Calvin held that the fourth commandment teaches neither the "one-day-in-seven" principle nor the obligation to set aside a specific day of the week, only that certain times be set aside in order that the worship of God may be maintained (p. 451).

16. Schaff, *Creeds*, 3: 68-70; from Part 2, Article 7 – *Of Ecclesiastical Power* (emphasis original in the fourth paragraph). Note that much of this treatment is conditioned by reaction to Roman Catholic abuses of the Lord's Day.

17. *Creeds*, 3: 161-63. The Lord's Day is probably in view in these statements; according to introductory remarks in Article 10, the propositions that follow are directed toward controversy among adherents of the Augsburg Confession "touching ecclesiastical ceremonies or rites, which are neither enjoined nor forbidden in the Word of God, but have been introduced into the church merely for the sake of order and seemliness" (pp. 160-61). As we have already seen, the Lord's Day is clearly included in the Augsburg Confession among

such "ecclesiastical ceremonies or·rites."

18. Article 24, "Coetus Sacra," *Creeds*, 3:227: "Coetus autem sacros sic peragendos esse censemus, ut ante omnia verbum Dei in publicum plebi quottidie proponatur, Scripturae abdita per idoneos ministros quottidie eruantur edisseranturque: sacra Eucharistia celebranda piorum subinde fides exerceatur, precationi pro omnibus omnium necessitatibus assidue instetur."

19. ed. A. Cochrane, *Reformed Confessions of the 16th Century* (Philadelphia: Westminster, 1966), p. 291 (editor's captions omitted; Latin original, *Creeds*, 3: 298; for an alternative English translation, p. 899). The judgment of Bauckham (*From Sabbath to Lord's Day*, p. 318, followed by A. Lincoln, p. 393), made on the basis of Bullinger's *Decades* as well as the Second Helvetic Confession, that he "wholly changed Calvin's emphasis" misreads the evidence and overstates the differences between them.

20. *Creeds*, 3: 376-77. This is the only section that can be plausibly construed as in some way pertinent to the Sabbath or Lord's Day question.

21. See Gilfillan, *The Sabbath*, pp. 417-446; particularly pp. 421-426.

Chapter 5

Summary and Evaluation

Summary

Calvin's teaching on the Sabbath or Lord's Day question may be summarized by the following set of propositions.

1. The Decalogue is a transcript of God's immutable moral law and is binding on humanity in all ages.

2. The fourth commandment, being one element in the Decalogue, is one of God's immutable laws and binding on humanity in all ages; in that sense the Sabbath institution (though not necessarily weekly Sabbath observance) is a creation ordinance.

3. The Sabbath day required under the old dispensation by the fourth commandment was a type or figure of spiritual rest.

4. Spiritual rest is ceasing from our own sinful works, mortifying our old nature, so that God may perform his sanctifying work in us; it may also be defined as conforming to God's will or imitating him.

5. Observing the weekly Sabbath in the Old Testament did not simply involve ceasing from the labors of the other six days; that rest was to be used for public worship and private meditation on the promised reality such rest typified.

6. Since God was pleased to provide his people with a foretaste of the reality still only prefigured, the weekly Sabbath was a sign of an invisible grace; it was, therefore, a sacrament of regeneration.

7. At the coming of Christ, the light in whose presence all shadows disappear, spiritual rest became a full reality; consequently, the weekly Sabbath as a type and sacrament was abrogated.

8. Although the perfection of spiritual rest will not be realized until the eschatological Last Day, that rest is now an actual possession of the believer; spiritual rest, presently enjoyed, and eternal rest are the same in substance.

9. Christians, strictly speaking, are no longer obliged to keep a weekly day of rest; the relaxation of that demand, however, should not be understood as abrogating the fourth commandment but as intensifying and elevating its demands.

10. For Christians, keeping the Sabbath means, in the final analysis, experiencing the spiritual rest (freedom from sin, newness of life) they have by virtue of being buried and raised with Christ.

11. Such spiritual rest cannot be limited to one day of the week but must be practiced daily, perpetually.

12. The experience of spiritual rest necessarily expresses itself in deeds of piety and Christian service, meditation upon God's works, and acts of worship; since spiritual rest is perpetual, daily public worship is the ideal for Christians.

13. Since Christians are subject to the same sinful weakness as those under the old covenant, a practical necessity exists for certain stated times to be set aside so that believers, being released from worldly cares and distractions, might be free to meditate privately and to assemble publicly for worship.

14. The Jewish Sabbath was perfectly suited to meet that need, but because so much superstition became associated with it by

the failure to see that the typical·mystery had passed away with Christ, the ancient church substituted the Lord's Day for it; that substitution was particularly appropriate because it memorialized Christ's resurrection, the day on which the Old Testament figure ceased to exist.

15. Today the Lord's Day still serves the need it was designed to meet; in principle, however, those Christians cannot be condemned who may wish to set apart some other day or even to pattern their lives by some other arrangement than a weekly day of rest, as long as they keep in view the need for stated times of worship and meditation.

16. Christians, therefore, do not keep the Lord's Day because it has some religious significance (that is, because it is a divine requirement); rather, they observe it freely and voluntarily, solely out of a concern for harmony and order in the church.

17. The physical rest provided by the fourth commandment for servants and other laborers is extrinsic to the basic concerns of the precept; the rest of both Jewish Sabbath and Lord's Day is not an end in itself, but a means to the end of meditation and public worship.

18. This provision of rest does remind masters or employers that they must not inhumanly oppress those who are subject to their authority; that, however, is a consideration that, strictly speaking, belongs to the second table of the law rather than the first.

19. The core of the fourth commandment and the essence of the Sabbath institution is that the creature should be conformed to the Creator, and that such imitation should express itself in a life characterized by public worship and private meditation upon God's works.

Evaluation

Any assessment of Calvin's view of the Sabbath and his explanation of the fourth commandment needs to keep in view the observations made at the close of the previous chapter. For Calvin, like the other Reformers, matters relating to keeping the ten commandments, particularly the fourth, while surely important, were not their dominating concern.

It may be difficult for Christians today to appreciate fully the spiritual and intellectual turmoil the Reformers experienced in breaking with the Roman Catholic Church. At the same time, however, we can understand how those called to spend their lives in dispelling the centuries-long darkness that had engulfed truths that are the indispensable life source of Christianity, would not likely be as concerned with questions related primarily to a specific and less central aspect of piety. For Calvin, forced to spend an entire lifetime contending for a fully gracious salvation and the Scriptures as our sole authority in matters of doctrine and practice, the Sabbath question never received the attention it might have, nor was it subjected to the full force of his exegetical powers. In short (and at the risk of suggesting an ultimately false disjunction), his dominating preoccupation was gospel, not law.[1] The question of Lord's Day observance never was the issue for Calvin that it became to subsequent generations of Protestantism, especially in the Reformed tradition. Consequently, we should not expect a formulation from him in terms of later debates.

Understanding Calvin in terms of his milieu, however, is not the same as ascertaining the validity of his views. A viewpoint, with the factors that shape it, is one thing; whether or not it is true, quite another. The latter is our interest now. How do Calvin's views of the Sabbath institution and the fourth commandment stand in the light of Scripture?

In addressing that question here my primary concern is to note what seem to me to be certain deficiencies in his views. In that respect, my appraisal is one-sided and does not do justice to the value of so much that Calvin teaches for the church today.[2]

1. I begin with a consideration drawn from the nature of the Decalogue. The heart of the fourth commandment, Calvin says repeatedly, is the injunction to practice spiritual rest. Spiritual rest, he likewise makes abundantly clear, is perpetual cessation from sin so that God may perform his sanctifying work in us.

It is difficult to see any real difference between this notion of spiritual rest and Jesus' teaching, consonant with the rest of Scripture, about the summary of the whole law, including the ten commandments (e.g., Matt. 22:35-40). For Calvin, spiritual rest is ceasing from sin, and the positive side of such cessation is loving "the Lord your God with all your heart and with all your soul and with all your mind ... and ... your neighbor as yourself."

But, also according to the uniform teaching of Scripture, the Decalogue is a detailed declaration of God's law, the explicit kind of enunciation that sinners need, more generally summarized by the command to love God and neighbor. In other words, the particular elements of the Decalogue are related to Christ's love summary as species to genus, specific aspects to integrating whole.

Consequently, to attribute to any one of the ten commandments, the comprehensive force that properly belongs to Christ's summary effectively deprives that particular commandment of its intended place in the Decalogue. That is precisely what happens when Calvin discusses the fourth commandment. The notion of spiritual rest he finds there gives to it a basic force that it cannot have biblically; a part of the Decalogue receives the meaning divinely intended for the whole. Jonathan Edwards, for one, already grasped this point. In commenting on Calvin's views, he says, "And if it [the fourth commandment] stands in force now only as signifying a spiritual, Christian rest, and holy behavior at all times, it doth not remain as one of the ten commands, but as a summary of all the commands."[3]

It remains perplexing how Calvin, who elsewhere correctly formulates the relation of each element of the Decalogue to Christ's summary, could have failed to observe that distinction in discussing the fourth commandment. At any rate, he plainly does give it a force that properly belongs only to the summary of the Decalogue. He has overlooked its specific place in God's law and, consequently, missed its true meaning. This contention will be substantiated by a more direct examination of his views.

2. A basic error is Calvin's failure to reckon adequately with the Sabbath institution as a creation ordinance. Other deficiencies in his views are due to this fundamental defect. He did recognize, as we have seen, that the Sabbath is mandated at creation and, correlatively, that the fourth commandment is perpetually and universally binding.[4] But the creation Sabbath is not given sufficient attention; its meaning does not have the controlling place it must in determining a fully biblical notion of the Sabbath institution.

How substantially Calvin has missed biblical teaching about the Sabbath given at creation is easily seen in his notion of spiritual rest. This basic concern of the fourth commandment is to cease from our own sinful works in order that God may perform his sanctifying work. The six days of labor mentioned are seen as a reference to the works of sinful flesh.

Clearly, then, for Calvin the existence of sin and the consequent need for sanctification is indispensable to the basic thrust of the fourth commandment. In other words, the Sabbath institution has meaning only within the orbit of redemption. Considerations arising from the prefall institution of the Sabbath, where sin and (the need for) redemption are necessarily absent, could not be more effectively excluded.

Even in his commentary on Genesis 2:3, where we might reasonably expect some reference to the meaning of the Sabbath institution for Adam before the fall, discussion instead focusses on spiritual rest and the sinful weakness that requires certain times to be set aside for worship and meditation. The meaning of the Sabbath institution prior to the fall seems not to have crossed his mind.

This failure to reckon with the creation (prefall) Sabbath

explains the characteristic emphases in Calvin's view. Since he considers the Sabbath entirely within a context where sin is endemic, he finds nothing "positive" in the commandment's mention of six days of labor. Since the fall, all human efforts, of themselves sinful and worthless, deserve only divine condemnation. Accordingly, the command to rest on the seventh day is cut off from any positive correlation to the six days of work; these two elements can only be related antithetically, or the days of work viewed, at best, concessively.[5]

3. We are now able to see how Calvin arrived at the ideal of daily public worship. The mention of six days of labor is a recognition of sinful actions, not a command to engage in legitimate human callings or other cultural activity. The command to rest on the seventh day is the only positive precept. Further, such rest receives its definition from being antithetically related to the six days of work; it is rest from sin, in that sense, spiritual rest. In short, the core of the fourth commandment, on its negative side, may be summed up by saying, "Stop sinning."[6]

Spiritual rest finds outward expression in exercises of piety; mercy, kindness, and love of neighbor are its reflexes. Before the Lord, it expresses itself directly in acts of worship and devotion. But such rest, by the nature of the case, is to be enjoyed (we might also say, exercised) perpetually or not at all. So Calvin, with no other positive considerations in the fourth commandment to qualify the notion of spiritual rest he finds there, is left to conclude that public worship is to be constant. As the heart of spiritual rest, it may not be confined to any one day of week but should be practiced daily.

Still, in the Old Testament economy this commandment obviously required the Jews to spend the seventh day of each week in worship and physical rest. That Calvin can only explain, as he does in the *Institutes* and elsewhere, by maintaining that the fourth commandment given to Moses at Sinai was an accommodation to sinful human inability to practice daily public worship. The ideal at the heart of the Sabbath ordinance was relaxed and modified out of consideration for the sinful weakness of the Jews, and also to show them typically (the seventh day of each week) the spiritual rest that would one day be brought by the promised Messiah. Similarly, Christians, although they no longer keep a typical Sabbath, observe the Lord's Day because they, like the Jews, are subject to the same sinful weakness that prohibits keeping the ideal Sabbath.

To highlight the central strand of our argument in the preceding paragraphs: Calvin's failure to take the command for six days of work positively fixes spiritual rest, and particularly the aspect of daily public worship, as the essential requirement of the fourth commandment.

Two further conclusions, implicit in the discussion to this point, may be accented. 1) Given Calvin's understanding of spiritual rest as the essence of the fourth commandment, Sabbath-keeping (the reflex of spiritual rest) must be practiced either perpetually or not at all. 2) Sabbath-keeping for Calvin is only meaningful in a context where sin is a reality.[7]

4. The greatest difficulty with Calvin's view of the fourth commandment, then, is this: If he takes all its language positively (the working in view, as well as the rest), he is faced with making sin an integral element in one of God's eternal and immutable principles for governing his creation. It might be objected at this point that virtually all the other parts of the Decalogue contemplate a situation where sin is present. For instance, the sixth commandment presupposes the reality of murder. Even more basically, however, it also has in view the inherent sanctity of human life, made in God's image. That sanctity was certainly as true before the fall as it is after sin enters the scene. Similarly, the negative, sin-conditioned language of the seventh commandment reflects the ideal of chastity and sexual purity, an ideal with meaning even before the fall.

No similar line of reflection, however, is open to Calvin on the fourth commandment. He understands it as referring too pervasively to the postfall situation. In failing to see the positive connection between the days of work and the day of rest, he can find no meaning for it in anything other than a redemptive context. To be sure, the core of the commandment in his view, spiritual rest – understood as the imitation of God – does have meaning apart from sin. But that core, as I have tried to show, is a summary of the whole law and misses whatever may be the specific force of the commandment. The only instance where Calvin does anything approaching full justice to the language of the fourth commandment is in the case of Old Testament Israel: the people were to rest each week on the seventh day, after six days of labor; but the significance of that Sabbath rest is still entirely redemptive.[8]

Calvin's view of the fourth commandment, all told, impales him on the horns of a dilemma. On the one hand, when he deals with its specific language, the result is Sabbath-keeping with no meaning outside of the scope of redemption. On the other hand, when he states its core, that the creature is to imitate the creator, a notion with relevance apart from redemption, the result is equivalent to a summary of the whole law and so misses its specific force. Calvin is unable to do justice to the fourth commandment at its most basic level, as one among God's eternal and immutable principles for governing his creation and the unfolding of history.

5. My criticism to this point rests on the assumption that the Sabbath institution is a specific creation ordinance and that the essence of that ordinance is reflected in the fourth commandment. In other words, the commandment embodies a principle intended to govern human life and conduct both before and after the fall. Further, this principle is specific; within the Decalogue it is coordinate with the other nine commandments, and so subordinate, not identical, to Christ's summary of the law.

But is this assumption biblical and, if so, what are some of its implications? In taking up that question, a further observation about Calvin is in order.

One factor that influenced his view of the fourth

commandment is the belief that all types have been abolished by the earthly ministry of Christ. As we have seen, he emphasizes that point repeatedly. Consequently, he plainly has difficulty in accepting the fourth commandment, without qualification, as binding for all times and places. The precept obviously contains a typical element and so, he reasons, has in some sense been modified or its typical part abrogated with the advent of Christ. That conclusion, coupled with neglect of the significance of the creation Sabbath, influenced his thinking toward the idea of spiritual rest as the basic concern of the commandment.

How ought we to evaluate the notion that all types have been abolished with the coming of Christ? To raise that question here, I should be clear, is not to question that under the Old Testament economy, particularly for Israel as a theocracy, a body of types and symbols prefigured the ministry of Christ incarnate and so was abrogated by that ministry. The writer of Hebrews, for one, is emphatically clear on that point (e.g., 9:1-10:18). But what about typical elements in special revelation prior to the fall? Calvin's mind on that question is difficult to know exactly, since, as far as I can tell, he does not address it directly. But from those places where he says that Christ has abolished all types by his coming it seems likely that he includes all types, prefall, preredemptive, if any, as well as redemptive.[9]

6. Whatever Calvin's view may be, the notion that every preredemptive type has ceased to function with the coming of Christ runs counter to biblical considerations that come to light in a passage like 1 Corinthians 15:44-49.[10]

The immediate context (vv. 42-49) contrasts the bodies of believers before and after the resurrection. The former, subject to the ravages of sin (cf. Rom. 5:12ff.), is mortal, dishonorable, and weak; the latter is marked by immortality, glory, and strength (vv. 42-43). The one, in a word, is "psychical" (ψυχικόν), the other, "Spiritual" (πνευματικόν, v. 44a).[11] But beginning in the middle of verse 44, it appears, the contrast broadens, on the one side, to include the original creation body as well as the body effected by sin. In other words, the ultimate preeschatological counterpart to the eschatological, resurrection body is the *prefall* body of Genesis 2:7 (cited in v. 45).

Is this a correct reading of verses 44b-45? Does Paul in fact include the prefall, creation body with the body in need of redemption when he refers to the psychical body? Initially, that may seem to be finding more in these verses than is there.

The adjective "psychical" (ψυχικόν)[12] appears in the New Testament only six times[13] – in this passage (twice in v. 44, once in v. 46) and elsewhere in 1 Corinthians 2:14, James 3:15, and Jude 19. In each of the latter three instances, the notion of sin and what is conditioned by sin is clearly constitutive (in that sense, "natural"). In other words, any preredemptive (prefall) connotations are necessarily excluded. Apparently, then, the other three occurrences in 1 Corinthians 15, especially in view of Paul's use in 2:14, are limited to having the same, sin-conditioned force, excluding any preredemptive associations.

More careful reflection on the passage, however, brings us to a different conclusion. Verse 44a states no more than that the psychical body precedes the Pneumatic body, antithetically, in point of time. Verse 44b, however, adds the additional thought, "If there is a psychical body, then there is also a Spiritual body." The flat antithesis between the two bodies maintained up to this point (vv. 42-44a), is significantly modified; Paul now argues, in a direct, linear fashion, from the one body to the other. The psychical body does not simply precede the Spiritual, but, much more, anticipates it; the psychical body, by its very nature, implies the Pneumatic.

In verse 45, to support ("so also") the assertion of verse 44b, Paul cites Genesis 2:7 (with the interpretative glosses, "first" and "Adam"): "the first man Adam was made a living soul (ψυχὴν ζῶσαν)." Plainly, Adam by virtue of creation and before the fall is in view.

This use of Genesis 2:7 as support for the argument of verse 44b, together with what Paul goes on to say in the rest of verse 45, prompts a further observation. The psychical nature with which Adam was endowed · at creation anticipates the endowment of "life-giving Spirit" received by the second Adam, Christ, at his resurrection.[14]

Verse 46 confirms this observation. There Paul expands his outlook by introducing a generalizing principle that includes not only the body but its context or environment.[15] It is not the Pneumatic, the complete, the eschatological, that comes first in the unfolding of history. Rather, first comes the anticipatory, the prefiguring, the preeschatological order (the "psychical" order) and then, consequently, the Pneumatic or eschatological order; the first, original creation looks forward to the new and final creation. That is so even apart from the fall and human sin.

7. The teaching of these verses prompts us to draw from them the following three principles:

1) Creation was from the beginning and continues to be oriented toward eschatology; by its very constitution ("psychical") it anticipates the eschatological (the "Spiritual").

2) Since the first creation thus implies the eventual emergence of the new creation, typology is inherent in the original creation and therefore antedates the fall; the psychical is typical, prefiguring and anticipating the Pneumatic.[16]

3) Given the fall, redemption is the absolutely essential means for the psychical to come to its full realization in the Pneumatic; redemption, made necessary only because of the fall, leaves its imprint on the eschatological state.

Uniformly in Paul's theology, to expand briefly on the third principle, the Spiritual is constitutive of and so synonymous with the eschatological, because the Spirit is the giver of life. Verse 45 expresses that in a sweeping and christologically qualified fashion.[17] The realm of the Spirit is the eschatological realm because the Spirit is the source of (eschatological) life; the Spirit and life cannot be separated.

To speak of life brings into view another important strand of Paul's teaching. Throughout his writings, but notably in Romans 5:12ff., righteousness and life are inseparable. As an invariable rule, righteousness receives the verdict of justification, issuing in eternal life. In contrast, sin earns condemnation, resulting in death. On the positive side, then, righteousness is absolutely prerequisite for attaining eschatological life. The Pneumatic state is exponential of righteousness;[18] (consummate) righteousness is the indispensable basis for life and guarantees it.

It may now be clearer how the eschatological state, anticipated in the original creation order, has its complexion colored by redemption. To say that righteousness is the basis of the eschatological state is to say, as far as sinners are concerned, that Christ is the basis of the eschatological state; apart from him, sinners remain unrighteous. Moreover, only in Christ is found the confirmed and consummate righteousness on which the eternal state rests. Only as believers share in Christ's death and resurrection do they share in the life-giving Spirit, who raised him up.[19] For the sinner there is no life without redemption in Christ. The christological and the eschatological can never be separated. To be "in the Spirit" is to be "in Christ" (Rom. 8:9).

8. With these comments on typology in view we can reflect further on biblical teaching concerning the Sabbath. Basic is the notion of rest. The Sabbath, therefore, has eschatological significance. Calvin recognizes that in quoting Isaiah 66:23 to show that the Sabbath will not be fully celebrated until the Last Day. The eschatological reference of the Sabbath is also implied in passages which teach that Israel's Sabbath was a sign of sanctification (Ezek. 20:12-20; Exod. 31:13-17). Sanctification, as an ongoing process of personal renewal in righteousness, reaches its ultimate realization in the eschatological realm of the Spirit, where all righteousness finds its consummate expression.

Several themes in the teaching of Jesus, to take one New Testament example, provide further insight into the eschatological nature of the Sabbath institution in the unfolding of revelation. In John's Gospel, particularly, he presents salvation as an offer of life (e.g., 6:35; 11:25; 14:6) – an inherently Spiritual, eschatological reality (cf. 6:63), as we have already noted.[20]

Similarly, his proclamation of redemption is an offer of freedom (John 8:32, 36), peace (John 14:27), and, of special interest for this study, rest (Matt. 11:28-20). All these notions of salvation/redemption – life, freedom, peace, and rest – are coordinate facets of consummate blessing. Each finds its supreme realization in the eschatological realm. Sabbath rest, therefore, is ultimately related to and characterizes the order of the Spirit.

9. Given both the typology inherent in the original creation and the eschatological reference of the Sabbath, the following picture of the prefall Sabbath emerges. Genesis 2:2-3, together with their commentary in the fourth commandment, show that the weekly Sabbath given to Adam served a function in the creaturely realm similar to the seventh day of the creation week for the Creator. As God rested from his completed work of creation, so man would enter into his rest after completing his God-given tasks as vicegerent over the creation (cf. Heb. 4:10). This analogy between Creator and image-bearing creature involves an important difference. The creating work of God had been completed and his rest begun (cf. Heb. 4:3b-4). The task entrusted to Adam/man had yet to be performed; his rest was still future (cf. Heb. 4:9).

What exactly was the task incumbent on Adam? Traditionally, Reformed theology has formulated it in terms of the obligation to obey certain commands of a cultic and cultural nature, with the specific prohibition of eating the forbidden fruit, so that he/humanity might be confirmed in a state of righteousness (the covenant of works). Now confirmed righteousness, as we have noted, issues in life, the realm of the Spirit, the eschatological order. So, in terms of 1 Corinthians 15:44b-45, Adam's task may be understood as the obligation, by means of successful probation, to raise the pre-eschatological, psychical order to the eschatological order,[21] which it anticipates. As Vos puts it:

> The only reasonable interpretation of the Genesis-account (*e mente Pauli*) is this, that provision was made and probation was instituted for a still higher state, both ethico-religiously and physically complexioned, than was at that time in the possession of man. In other words the eschatological complex and prospect were there in the purpose of God from the beginning.[22]

Adam's weekly Sabbath, then, involved two basic, interrelated facets. On the one hand, eschatological Sabbath-rest was a still future goal; he had work to do. At the same time, he was not to think that his labors were meaningless, submerged in an endless historical flow. He was to toil, but that toil would result in rest. A weekly day of rest was instituted to remind him of the purposefulness of his work; it also provided rhythmic refreshment of body and soul (periodic psycho-physical rest, in other words), appropriate to him in the integrity of his psychical nature. The weekly Sabbath was a continual reminder to Adam that history is not a ceaseless repetition of days. Rather, at the beginning of each week he could look forward to the rest of the seventh day. That weekly cycle impressed on him that he, together with the created order as a whole, was moving toward a goal, a nothing less than eschatological culmination.

Seen in this light, the creation Sabbath was the preeminent type of the prefall period. The psychical rest of each week prefigured the ultimate, eschatological goal of the whole created order and, at the same time, emphasized its present state of pre-eschatological incompleteness. This conclusion prompts at least two related observations.

1) The language of the fourth commandment does not suggest anything but a positive correlation between the six days of labor and the seventh day of rest. In fact, that latter is unintelligible without the former and vice versa; the day of rest gives meaning to and, in turn, receives its meaning from the six

days of labor. The seven day week is a divinely ordained whole; it implies a philosophy of history that even the most unreflective mind can intuit.[23]

The primary concern of the fourth commandment is not pragmatic – to provide time for public and private worship and religious instruction. Rather, the original concern of the weekly Sabbath continues. It is for restful reflection on our lives, before God, in view of the ultimate outcome of history, when the present psychical order will be transformed into the Spiritual; it is for reviewing our cultural calling and activities of the past six days in that eschatological light. This is not at all to imply that cultic elements do not have a proper, even integral, place on the Sabbath. Indeed, such worship is crucial and ought to be prominent, especially in the postfall Sabbath, when believers must focus attention on Christ, rather than themselves, as the one who for them has fulfilled the command for six days of labor and in whom they are fulfilling that command (e.g., 1 Cor. 15:58; Rev. 14:13; 19:7-8). Where the Sabbath institution is properly appreciated and functions as it should, cultural concerns and avocations, on the one hand, and cultic activities, on the other, are neither confused nor polarized.

Vos is worth quoting at length here:

From what has been said about the typical, sacramental meaning of the Sabbath it follows that it would be a mistake to base its observance primarily on the ground of utility. The Sabbath is not the outcome of an abnormal state of affairs in which it is impossible, apart from the appointment of a fixed day, to devote sufficient care to the religious interests of life. On such a view it might be maintained that for one sufficiently at leisure to give all his time to the cultivation of religion the keeping of the Sabbath would no longer be obligatory. Some of the continental Reformers, out of reaction to the Romish system of holy days, reasoned after this fashion. But they reasoned wrongly. The Sabbath is not in the first place a means of advancing religion. It has its main significance apart from that, in pointing forward to the eternal issues of life and history. Even the most advanced religious spirit cannot absolve itself from partaking in that. It is a serious question whether the modern church has not too much lost sight of this by making the day well-nigh exclusively an instrument of religious propaganda, at the expense of its eternity-typifying value. Of course it goes without saying that a day devoted to the remembrance of man's eternal destiny cannot be properly observed without the positive cultivation of those religious concerns which are so intimately joined to the final issue of his lot. But, even where this is conceded, the fact remains that it is possible to crowd too much into the day that is merely subservient to religious propaganda, and to void it too much of the static, God-ward and heavenly-ward directed occupation of piety.[24]

2) The distinctiveness of the weekly Sabbath as a type needs to be appreciated. We should ponder that the entire sum of eschatological considerations, the fulness of consummate blessing, is comprehended under a figure (rest) that, strictly speaking, typifies just one element of that Pneumatic state of affairs. Despite coordination with other elements such as peace, freedom, and even life, rest, eschatologically considered, has a prominence of its own. When the difference between the psychical and the Spiritual – the contrast between the anticipatory and prefiguring character of the former and the permanence and perpetuity of the latter – is to be highlighted, (psychical) rest does that most aptly. That is why, at creation, the weekly Sabbath was made the comprehensive, all-inclusive type it is. Rest, more than anything else, reflects the permanence and perfection of the Pneumatic state. Rest points to that state where no more (pre-eschatological) work is necessary, because nothing remains to be perfected. It pictures the ultimate realization of the entire scope of eschatological interests.

10. We may now consider in more detail than we so far have the effects of the fall upon the Sabbath institution or, in other words, the relation of the creation Sabbath to the redemptive Sabbath. Above all, the fall does not abrogate either the creation Sabbath or its typical function. The psychical creation still anticipates the

Pneumatic creation, albeit with the added burden of sin and its corrupting consequences (Rom. 8:19-22). Man is no longer capable of living up to the demands of the fourth commandment (work and rest) or, for that matter, any other of God's commands. The task of bringing the psychical creation to its eschatological fulfillment has been taken from him and given to the better and more worthy Servant. The Father has begun, through the redemptive work of his Son, to bring history to its climax. The second and last Adam takes up the task forfeited by the first Adam.

The history of redemption undoubtedly began to have an effect on the Sabbath institution soon after the fall. That impact on the weekly Sabbath is apparent in the theocracy, an impact that Calvin readily saw. What is not so apparent in analyzing the Mosaic Sabbath, however, is the distinction between the fourth commandment as it reflects a universally binding creation ordinance and what in the commandment was peculiar to its Old Covenant administration. That distinction, it appears, Calvin did not always observe, particularly when he argues that the typical element in the fourth commandment has been abrogated.

There is validity, of course, in Calvin's idea that the Jewish Sabbath typified the spiritual rest[25] brought by Christ. That has to be so because all the forms and rituals of Old Testament religion, instituted after the fall and especially at Sinai, anticipated the work of Christ. On the other hand, it is plainly less than biblical, as I have already argued, for Calvin to view spiritual rest generically, equivalent, in general, to freedom from sin and its positive counterpart, love of God and neighbor. Spiritual rest, typified under the Mosaic economy by the Sabbath and fulfilled by Christ, has its sense in terms of the specific issues and concerns of the fourth commandment. The spiritual, redemptive rest already brought by Christ assures believers of the eventual future realization of the eschatological rest typified by the creation Sabbath. It does so by granting them to share in the perfect righteousness of Christ, on which basis the Spirit is now at work in them, preparing them for the consummate enjoyment of all the blessings of that rest. Spiritual rest in Christ is a foretaste in this life of the eschatological blessings subsequently to be enjoyed in their fulness.[26] Accordingly, we may properly speak of the abolition of the *Jewish* Sabbath at the coming of Christ,[27] in the sense that the *purely redemptive typical* element that had become associated with it under the Old Covenant, distinguishing it from the New Covenant Sabbath, has been abrogated. Spiritual rest, as it has become a reality in Christ, is no longer typified by the weekly Sabbath.

The relation between the creation and redemptive Sabbaths may be further clarified along the following lines.

1) The weekly Sabbath instituted at creation is a type of eschatological rest. But, as we have also seen, as such and more concretely, it points to the order of the Spirit in its perfect, consummate finality. It therefore continues to serve a typical function until what it prefigures is realized. That eschatological consummation, 1 Corinthians 15, for one, makes clear, will not be until the resurrection of the body (vv. 42-49), until the time "when he [Christ] hands over the kingdom to God the Father ..., so that God may be all in all" (vv. 24-28).

Certainly, believers have already received the Spirit as an actual deposit on their eschatological inheritance (Eph. 1:14); the blessings they enjoy are "semi-eschatological." But to reason, on the basis of these incipiently enjoyed blessings, that the weekly Sabbath has ceased, reflects a greatly impoverished view of biblical eschatology. To conclude that the Sabbath institution has been abrogated because all the blessings of the eschatological order are in principle realized in the New Testament church, as if nothing essentially new remains to be realized, is to lose sight of the present incomprehensibility of the consummate glory of the new heavens and new earth that God, in Christ and through the Spirit, has prepared for his people, glory that neither eye has seen nor ear heard (1 Cor. 2:9). The weekly Sabbath is the type of that still future perfection and will continue to picture it until it becomes reality.

2) The Old Covenant redemptive Sabbath was not, strictly speaking, the Sabbath institution expressed in the fourth commandment, but the particular expression that creation ordinance took in redemptive history from the fall until Christ. Since the redemptive considerations it typified have been fulfilled in Christ, it is no longer in force. That fulfillment, however, has left an indelible imprint on the creation Sabbath. The fulfillment of the redemptive Sabbath was absolutely indispensable to realizing the ultimate outcome in view, typically, in the creation Sabbath. Without the redemptive rest brought by Christ, Spiritual rest would be an unobtainable goal for sinners. Confirmed redemption rest, achieved by Christ for believers, is their guarantee of the full realization of the eschatological rest in view already in the creation Sabbath.[28]

To give a concluding focus to much of the preceding discussion, Scripture teaches that the weekly Sabbath was a creation ordinance and that it was given as the type par excellence of the eschatological state toward which creation is moving. To be sure, the realization of that Spiritual order cannot now be realized, given the fall, apart from redemption. But to fail to see the significance of the creation Sabbath before the fall and apart from redemption, is to render the fourth commandment largely meaningless. Calvin's view is a clear illustration of that failure.

The typical element is a permanent aspect of the fourth commandment. The Lord's Day, as the weekly Sabbath, remains a type until the present created order (the psychical) gives way to one that is consummately higher and better (the Pneumatic). To say that believers are still bound to keep this type is not to compromise the freedom brought by Christ. Rather, observing the Lord's Day is an expression of that freedom. The weekly rest day, faithfully kept by the church, is a concrete witness to a watching world that Christians are not enmeshed in the turmoil of an impersonal historical process but look with confidence to sharing in the consummation of God's purposes for the creation, a witness that there does indeed remain an eschatological Sabbath-rest for the people of God (Heb. 4:9).[29]

11. Finally, a brief evaluation of the possible notion that the Christian Sabbath is sacramental in the sense that, along with baptism and the Lord's Supper, it is virtually a third sacrament.[30]

The Sabbath is not a sacrament of the new covenant in the full sense for the following reasons.

1) If the Sabbath is a sacrament, then it should be observed only by believers. Rules similar to those Paul gives respecting the Lord's Supper (1 Cor. 11:17ff.) ought to regulate Sabbath keeping. In other words, unbelievers should be warned against observing the Sabbath to avoid bringing condemnation on themselves. The complete anomaly of that scenario ought to be apparent. To view the Sabbath as a sacrament implies not only that a part of humanity is exempt from the obligation to keep one of the commandments of God's immutable and universally binding law, but also that non-Christians are positively to be encouraged in breaking that law. This difficulty, it appears to me, is insurmountable; it cannot be gotten around by any amount of biblically-based reasoning.

2) If the Sabbath is a sacrament of the new covenant, then its meaning lies solely within the orbit of redemption, as do baptism and the Lord's Supper. But to draw that conclusion entails denying, contrary to Scripture, that the Sabbath is a creation ordinance.

3) The teaching of 1 Corinthians 15:45-49 makes clear certain implications of holding that the Sabbath is a sacrament of the new covenant. For one, to take that view would mean that, to those who observe it, the Sabbath seals what it signifies.

The weekly Sabbath typifies/signifies the perfection of the Pneumatic state. Even when that is granted, however, the distinctiveness of the Sabbath's typical function can be overlooked or misunderstood. That can happen all the more easily because eschatological perfection is inseparable from any redemptive manifestation of the Spirit. So, when we consider, for instance, that believers, already, in this life, have received the Spirit as the actual deposit on their eschatological inheritance (2 Cor. 1:22; Eph. 1:14), we may be inclined to conclude, in the light of that present possession, that the Sabbath is its sacramental sign and seal.

The distinctiveness of the Sabbath as a type, however, can not be found in any such semi-eschatological considerations. The weekly Sabbath is a type of the Pneumatic state in its absolute perfection, a state of perfection that is fully eschatological, where not even a single noneschatological vestige remains. In terms of the fundamental distinction of 1 Corinthians 15:44, a distinction with its roots, as we have seen, in the original, prefall creation order, the Sabbath points to the situation where the psychical creation will have been entirely transformed into the Pneumatic creation.

That state of affairs, signified by the Sabbath, does not yet exist. It will not arrive, as this passage teaches, until the resurrection of the body at Christ's return, until, at that time, the entire creation, along with believers, is delivered from its present groaning futility and bondage to decay (Rom. 8:19-23), until the day of the Lord arrives in all its cataclysmically transforming upheavals (2 Pet. 3:3-13). The catastrophic is necessary to bring in the purely Pneumatic. No matter how much is effected by the transforming power of the Spirit in this life, believers will still not be equipped to enjoy the blessings of the eternal Sabbath until they themselves have experienced personally the nothing less than apocalyptic transformation (bodily resurrection) that ushers in that Sabbath. The fulness of blessing the weekly Sabbath signifies cannot be sealed to those still with a psychical nature. So, both in view of the overall flow of redemptive history (the "already-not yet" structure of eschatological fulfillment in Christ) as well as the present (psychical) condition of believers within that flow, it should be clear how thoroughly inappropriate it is to view the Sabbath as a sacrament of the new covenant.

To find a sacramental element in the Sabbath misses its

significance in the economy of revelation. So far as the church is concerned, it is there each week as a constant reminder that no matter what heights of redemptive blessing are experienced in this life, the new heavens and earth to come will arrive with a splendor and glory beyond the imagination of the most sanctified believer. The Sabbath is there to remind us that the rich and full blessings we now enjoy in Christ will, by comparison, appear insignificant to those we will possess "when he appears, [and] we shall be like him, for we shall see him as he is" (1 John 3:2). About that comparison Calvin would surely agree.

References

1. This is a particularly risky way of putting things for Calvin, who among the major Reformers perhaps most clearly maintained the "third use" of the law (the positive role of the law as a guide to the believer for daily living). In fact, he calls it "the principal use, which pertains more closely to the proper purpose of the law ..." (*Institutes*, 1:360 [2:7:12]).

2. For a further elaboration of lines along which this critique unfolds, see my "Westminster and the Sabbath," forthcoming in a symposium commemorating the 350th anniversary of the completion of the work of the Westminster Assembly. There I also defend the validity, assumed here, of the three-fold distinction between moral, ceremonial, and judicial laws, held by Calvin and subsequently adopted in chapter 19 of *The Westminster Confession of Faith*.

3. *Works*, 3 (London: 1834): 95; quoted in J. Bannerman, *The Church of Christ*, 1 (Edinburgh: T&T Clark, 1868): 401.

4. It is perhaps worth recalling here the concluding words of his comments on Genesis 2:3: "... but inasmuch as it was commanded to men from the beginning that they might employ themselves in the worship of God, it is right that it should continue to the end of the world" (*Commentaries on Genesis*, 1: 107).

5. The way Calvin construes the language of the commandment is questionable. In his view, the six days of labor are a fact; the rest on the seventh day, on the other hand, is a command. His meaning is fairly paraphrased as follows: "you are laboring for six days and doing all

your work, but the seventh day is a Sabbath to the Lord your God; in it you shall not do any work ...." In the Hebrew text (both Exod. 20:9-10 and Deut. 5:13-14) the three verbs in question, "laboring," "doing" (work), and not "doing" (work), all have the same stem and tense (qal imperfect), which can be used as an imperative, though generally it has an indicative force. In this instance, in other words, Calvin takes the first two verbs, referring to the six days of labor, as indicatives, but the third, for resting on the seventh day, as an imperative. This reading, while there is nothing that excludes it grammatically, is unlikely; certainly it cannot be insisted on. The three verbs, in close conjunction, are syntactically parallel. Accordingly, apart from some contrary indication in the text, such as appears to be lacking here, all three verbs have the same force. Since the third (not working) can only be an imperative, so, too, the other two are most likely imperatives. But that conclusion is unacceptable to Calvin; it would leave him faced with the intolerable consequence of introducing an exhortation to sin into one of God's commandments.

6. This reinforces the observation above that in viewing the fourth commandment as enjoining spiritual rest, Calvin in effect makes it a summary of the whole law.

7. That does not mean that Calvin cannot hold something approximating to Sabbath-keeping (spiritual rest) for Adam before the fall. The spiritual rest enjoined in the fourth commandment, however, must always be seen against the background of existing sin. Rest, strictly speaking, implies cessation from something, and he is quite clear that in the commandment that "something" is sinful works.

8. Even here he considers the six days of labor a concession to Israel (i.e., God required only a seventh of their time), rather than a divine commandment.

9. E.g., *Institutes*, 1:426 (2:9:3), 451-456 (2:11:2-6); 2:1433 (4:18:4).

10. The following exegetical reflections are heavily indebted to Geerhardus Vos, "The Eschatological Aspect of the Pauline Conception of the Spirit," *Biblical and Theological Studies* (New York: Scribners, 1912), pp. 231-34 [ed. R. Gaffin, Jr., *Redemptive History and Biblical Interpretation. The Shorter Writings of Geerhardus Vos* (Phillipsburg: Presbyterian and Reformed, 1980), pp. 105-07]; cf. *The Pauline Eschatology* (Grand Rapids: Baker, 1979

[1930]), pp. 169-70 (footnote 19). For my own fuller treatment of the passage, see *Resurrection and Redemption. A Study in Paul's Soteriology* (Phillipsburg: Presbyterian and Reformed, 1987 [1978]), pp. 78-92, esp. 81-83.

11. The adjective "spiritual" (lower case) too easily suggests what is inherently "immaterial" or "nonphysical." In order to avoid that misunderstanding, particularly serious here, where it is applied to the resurrection body, as well as to keep clear, what more careful exegesis is bound to conclude, that the Greek adjective in v. 44 has the activity of the Holy Spirit in view, I will capitalize the English, where appropriate, as well as "Pneumatic" (used interchangeably).

12. A satisfactory English translation of this adjective here is notoriously difficult, facing the apparently insurmountable challenge of not obscuring the obvious tie in the Greek text with the noun ("soul," "being," "person") in v. 45. The usual proposals, "natural" or "physical," are deficient, the latter downright misleading. From the normative viewpoint of the original creation, the sin-ravaged, mortal body is in fact "unnatural"; "physical," by virtue of the main contrast of the passage, leaves the seriously erroneous impression that the resurrection body, by contrast, is nonphysical or immaterial. Consequently, I have settled here for the transliteration, "psychical."

13. It is not found in the canonical portions of the Septuagint, and only once in the pseudepigrapha (4 Macc. 1:32).

14. Note that Paul is not saying that Adam's psychical nature looked forward to life-giving ρνεῦμα specifically in the way the Spirit became Christ's possession shared with believers, as if, necessarily, that were the *only* way the Pneumatic could have been realized. That would saddle Paul with the elsewhere thoroughly unbiblical notion that from the outset, prior to the fall, creation was inherently in need of redemption. Nothing more is in view here than the de facto means (the work of the incarnate Christ necessitated by the fall) by which the psychical has found its fulfillment in the Pneumatic.

15. The neuter singular substantives in v. 46 (τὸ πνευματικόν, τὸ ψυχικόν) are most likely generalizing expressions, after which it would be a mistake, missing the broadening already given to the contrast in verse 45 (between Adam and Christ as whole persons), to read an implied "body" (σῶμα). Note, too, that in the immediately

following verses (47-49) the basic contrast of the passage is continued in explicitly cosmological or, one could say, "environmental" terms ("heaven"/"earth"). Elsewhere in Paul, Romans 8:20-22 especially intimates the cosmic dimension of future eschatological renewal.

16. Further confirmation for this principle may be found in Paul's statement elsewhere that Adam is a "type" or "pattern" (τύπος) of Christ (Rom. 5:14). M. Kline ("The Intrusion and the Decalogue," *Westminster Theological Journal*, 16, 1 (Nov. 1953): 1-22) argues that typology is a postfall phenomenon, confined to the covenant of grace. He defines typology in terms of the notion of intrusion that he develops (p. 6), and outlaws appeal to this verse for a prefall typology, on the basis that it proves no more than the relationship between Adam and Christ as federal heads. It appears to me, however, that to recognize that they are federal heads in God's dealings with humanity, concedes the point he denies. Neither Adam nor Christ can be dissociated from the ultimate outcome of their respective tasks as federal heads. In the terms of 1 Corinthians 15:45-49, Adam, in his representative capacity, was endowed with a psychical nature whose eschatological destiny he failed to achieve but rather, by his sin, subjected to pollution and decay. Christ, in contrast, has achieved what Adam forfeited; he has secured for himself and those he represents the eschatological destiny of the original psychical nature: consequent on the fall and redemption, a Pneumatic nature. Both are endowed with a psychical nature – Adam by creation, Christ by incarnation – but only Christ succeeds to the state that nature anticipates. Adam as a psychical being, then, is typical of Christ as a Pneumatic being.

17. Cf. Romans 7:6; 8:2, 11; 2 Corinthians 3:6, 17. (There is no more fundamental eschatological reality than life, in the ultimate, eternal sense.)

18. Vos, "Eschatology and the Spirit," p. 236.

19. This is likely Paul's thought in Romans 4:25: Christ "was raised again for our justification." In raising up the Son, the Father demonstrated the righteousness of the Son accomplished in his messianic capacity. The resurrection was thus a de facto justification. For believers to share in Christ's resurrection implies sharing in both the ground and goal of the justification his resurrection implies, that is, sharing in both confirmed righteousness (imputed, Rom. 5:18-19, as well as inwrought, Rom. 6:2ff, 15ff.), and eschatological life.

20. It is worth observing here that the "eternal life" so characteristic of John's Gospel and 1 John (3:15-16; 5:24; 6:27; 1 John 2:25, passim) is not "eternal" in the sense of being above or beyond history, "timeless" in some ahistorical sense, but because it has been revealed at the end of history and comes to believers out of that consummation; eternal life is eschatological life.

21. Which, in view of the fall and redemption in Christ, is the de facto Pneumatic order.

22. *The Pauline Eschatology*, p. 304.

23. A basic weakness in Calvin's view, as we have seen, is the failure to see this positive correlation. Even were it to be granted that the fourth commandment only applies in the context of redemption, it remains puzzling how he finds a contrast between our sinful works and the rest that God commands (or, at best, a concessive relationship between our work and the rest commanded). Since the fall sinners are no more capable of rest acceptable to God than they are of performing acceptable works.

24. *Biblical Theology* (Grand Rapids: Eerdmans, 1959), p. 157. Though Calvin is not named, a critique of his views, among others (as one of "the continental Reformers" mentioned), seems unmistakable.

25. I use this expression here and subsequently in Calvin's sense, unless otherwise noted.

26. Note, especially, Paul's metaphors for the present activity of the Spirit in believers: "down payment" (2 Cor. 1:22; 5:5; Eph. 1:14) and "firstfruits" (Rom. 8:23). Vos calls this state of affairs – already present in part, not yet in fulness – "semi-eschatological" (*The Pauline Eschatology*, p. 38); more usual designations are "realized" or "inaugurated eschatology."

27. As does Paul, Galatians 4:10,11; Colossians 2:16,17.

28. These considerations, to my mind, provide the most satisfying rationale for the change of the weekly Sabbath from the seventh day to the first. The guaranteed realization of the eschatological Sabbath, by the fulfillment of the redemptive (old covenant typical) Sabbath, marks a significant turn in history. In Christ the ultimate goal of the created process, typified by the creation Sabbath, is assured; the probationary element is no longer present. Specifically, Christ's resurrection is the signal event of such certainty achieved, so that the day of the week on which it occurred is now appropriately the day of

rest. The day that points to that consummate state is now enjoyed at the beginning of the week rather than at the end, thereby indicating that the goal of creation is now certain and no longer a matter of probation.

29. For a treatment of the Sabbath theology of Hebrews, see my "A Sabbath Rest Still Awaits the People of God," in *Pressing Toward the Mark. Essays Commemorating Fifty Years of the Orthodox Presbyterian Church* (ed. C. Dennison and R. Gamble; Philadelphia: the Committee for the Historian of the Orthodox Presbyterian Church, 1986), pp. 33-51 (including a critique of Calvin's interpretation of 4:10, p. 45).

30. Although I am unaware of anyone who actually argues this view, I take it up here as a potential view, toward which some may be disposed, and in order to highlight and clarify some of the conclusions already reached in this chapter.

SCRIPTURE INDEX

PERSONS INDEX

THEMATIC INDEX

Reformed Theological Writings
R. A. Finlayson

This volume contains a selection of doctrinal studies, divided into three sections:

General theology
The God of Israel; God In Three Persons; God the Father; The Person of Christ; The Love of the Spirit in Man's Redemption; The Holy Spirit in the Life of Christ; The Messianic Psalms; The Terminology of the Atonement; The Ascension; The Holy Spirit in the Life of the Christian; The Assurance of Faith; The Holy Spirit in the Life of the Church; The Church – The Body of Christ; The Authority of the Church; The Church in Augustine; Disruption Principles; The Reformed Doctrine of the Sacraments; The Theology of the Lord's Day, The Christian Sabbath; The Last Things.

Issues Facing Evangelicals
Christianity and Humanism; How Liberal Theology Infected Scotland; Neo-Orthodoxy; Neo-Liberalism and Neo-Fundamentalism; The Ecumenical Movement; Modern Theology and the Christian Message.

The Westminster Confession of Faith
The Significance of the Westminster Confession; The Doctrine of Scripture in the Westminster Confession of Faith; The Doctrine of God in the Westminster Confession of Faith; Particular Redemption in the Westminster Confession of Faith; Efficacious Grace in the Westminster Confession of Faith; Predestination in the Westminster Confession of Faith; The Doctrine of Man in the Westminster Confession of Faith.

R. A. Finlayson was for many years the leading theologian of the Free Church of Scotland and one of the most effective preachers and speakers of his time; those who were students in the 1950s deeply appreciated his visits to Christian Unions and IVF conferences. This volume contains posthumously edited theological lectures which illustrate his brilliant gift for simple, logical and yet warm-hearted presentation of Christian doctrine (I Howard Marshall).

272 pages   ISBN 1 85792 259 X   large format

MENTOR TITLES

Creation and Change by Douglas Kelly (large format, 272 pages)
A scholarly defence of the literal seven-day account of the creation of all things as detailed in Genesis 1. The author is Professor of Systematic Theology in Reformed Theological Seminary in Charlotte, North Carolina, USA.

The Healing Promise by Richard Mayhue (large format, 288 pages)
A clear biblical examination of the claims of Health and Wealth preachers. The author is Dean of The Master's Seminary, Los Angeles, California.

Puritan Profiles by William Barker (hardback, 320 pages)
The author is Professor of Church History at Westminster Theological Seminary, Philadelphia, USA. In this book he gives biographical profiles of 54 leading Puritans, most of whom were involved in the framing of the Westminster Confession of Faith.

Creeds, Councils and Christ by Gerald Bray (large format, 224 pages)
The author, who teaches at Samford University, Birmingham, Alabama, explains the historical circumstances and doctrinal differences that caused the early church to frame its creeds. He argues that a proper appreciation of the creeds will help the confused church of today.

MENTOR COMMENTARIES

1 and 2 Chronicles by Richard Pratt (hardback, 512 pages)
The author is professor of Old Testament at Reformed Theological Seminary, Orlando, USA. In this commentary he gives attention to the structure of Chronicles as well as the Chronicler's reasons for his different emphases from that of 1 and 2 Kings.

Psalms by Alan Harman (hardback, 456 pages)
The author, now retired from his position as a professor of Old Testament, lives in Australia. His commentary includes a comprehensive introduction to the psalms as well as a commentary on each psalm.

Amos by Gray Smith (hardback, 400 pages)
Gary Smith, a professor of Old Testament in Bethel Seminary, Minneapolis, USA, exegetes the text of Amos by considering issues of textual criticism, structure, historical and literary background, and the theological significance of the book.

Christian Focus Publications publishes biblically-accurate books for adults and children. The books in the adult range are published in three imprints.

Christian Heritage contains classic writings from the past.

Christian Focus contains popular works including biographies, commentaries, doctrine, and Christian living.

Mentor focuses on books written at a level suitable for Bible College and seminary students, pastors, and others; the imprint includes commentaries, doctrinal studies, examination of current issues, and church history.

For a free catalogue of all our titles, please write to
Christian Focus Publications,
Geanies House, Fearn,
Ross-shire, IV20 1TW, Great Britain

For details of our titles visit us on our web site
http://www.christianfocus.com